Annales Anglais
Concours Scientifiques 2017
La Fée Prépa

Auteurs

Quentin Cobweb

Delphine Mélusin

Professeurs agrégés d'anglais en CPGE dans un lycée parisien

anciens élèves de l'ENS de Fontenay -Saint-Cloud

membres de jurys de concours

publiant par modestie sous un pseudonyme

DEDICACE

A Albane et à ses parents

SOMMAIRE

AVANT-PROPOS

L'esprit des Annales de *La Fée Prépa* : permettre des progrès effectifs

De nombreuses années d'enseignement en CPGE – et par là donc de correction de copies de préparationnaires – nous ont appris une vérité bonne à savoir pour nos lecteurs : quel que soit le niveau de départ en anglais d'un étudiant, ce niveau s'améliore grandement à mesure que l'étudiant est amené à produire de l'écrit. En clair, même si vous êtes faible ou moyen en anglais, vos progrès entre le devoir 1 et le devoir 10 seront obligatoirement très sensibles, voire spectaculaires, et ce sans lien nécessaire avec les connaissances que vous aurez acquises entre temps par d'autres exercices comme la lecture. Lire, apprendre, c'est bien. Mais **faire,** c'est essentiel, surtout depuis le changement de format en langues des concours scientifiques. C'est en forgeant qu'on devient forgeron. Plus on fait de synthèses, mieux on fait les synthèses. Eh oui, c'est comme ça.

Pendant vos années de préparation aux concours, vous produirez grâce à vos professeurs d'anglais un certain nombre de devoirs qui seront corrigés, commentés, et vous aideront à progresser. Nous vous proposons de doubler, voire de tripler la dose, mais en vous corrigeant vous-même, sachant que si la note et les commentaires sur la copie sont importants, le plus important est que vous ayez fait le devoir, puis le suivant, et encore un autre. C'est un peu comme en sport, le chrono du jour compte, l'appréciation de l'entraîneur aussi, mais en dernière analyse, ce qui fait accomplir les progrès et permet à la performance finale – la seule qui importe réellement – d'être la meilleure possible, c'est votre entraînement régulier.

Pour optimiser le ratio temps passé/profit, nous vous proposons donc de travailler seul(e) sur les sujets du présent ouvrage, à votre rythme, mais en respectant toutefois les petits conseils que nous vous donnons ci-après. Cela ne vous prendra que quelques heures par mois (regroupées) pour un grand profit, si vous savez vous organiser. Le corrigé doit vous servir à mesurer vous-même la valeur approximative de votre travail. Souvenez-vous que l'évaluation chiffrée n'apporte rien à vos progrès, comparée à l'entraînement lui-même.

Donc, pendant votre temps libre, pendant les vacances par exemple, faites un sujet, puis un autre pendant le demi-semestre. Vous verrez vite que votre aisance dans les exercices requis s'améliore. Il y a à la fin du présent ouvrage un lien vers le site de La Fée Prépa, où vous trouverez des mises à jour gratuites, des sujets inédits et un formulaire de contact pour toutes vos remarques et questions.

Bon courage et bonne chance à toutes et à tous pour les concours 2017.

Conseils sur la méthode de travail

Pour tirer le meilleur profit de votre travail sur ces annales, nous vous conseillons de **procéder de manière progressive**, comme suit:

Faites pour commencer **tous les sujets des concours 2016** pour vous imprégner de l'esprit des épreuves, et ce, sans préjuger des concours que vous visez en priorité. Tous les sujets que vous ferez vous feront progresser. Vous vous accoutumerez en outre au format des épreuves, qui sont variables.

Travaillez ensuite **sur les sujets inédits "n°1"** de nos annales, sans respecter les conditions du concours, mais au contraire en vous donnant un peu de temps. Faites-les par exemple pendant les vacances ou le week-end. La meilleure technique au départ est de bien lire et relire les textes des dossiers de synthèse un jour, puis de les relire une dernière fois le matin suivant avant de commencer à composer. Faites un premier jet, puis faites une petite pause et revenez à votre devoir pour peaufiner.

En revanche, par la suite, plus vous aurez fait de sujets, plus vous devrez travailler vite. Quand vous arriverez aux **sujets "n°3" de nos annales**, il faudra travailler dans les conditions du concours. Bloquez une matinée ou un après-midi et faites tout le sujet en conditions de concours, sans vous laisser distraire. Consultez le corrigé et faites votre auto-évaluation le lendemain seulement, vous aurez davantage de distance critique.

N' enchaînez pas les sujets d'entraînement en mode « *Je bosse mon anglais pendant trois jours à fond deux semaines avant les concours* », songez plutôt à réserver absolument quelques heures par mois toute l'année à partir de maintenant pour cela. Mettez par exemple dans votre planning deux ou trois sujets par mois, soit 2 ou 3 x 4 heures, et faites-les sérieusement.

Et lisez **les rapports des jurys**. Ils sont sur les sites des concours des différentes écoles. C'est indispensable. Pour les rapports 2016, consultez-le de préférence **après** avoir travaillé les sujets.

Si vous devez être fidèles d'une seule publication en langue anglaise, que ce soit *The Guardian*. C'est désormais, statistiquement la source n°1 des sujets de concours dans toutes les filières.

I. SUJETS DES CONCOURS 2016 ET CORRIGÉS

SUJET X-ENS 2016

ÉPREUVE ÉCRITE DE LANGUE VIVANTE

ANGLAIS

Durée totale de l'épreuve écrite de langue vivante (A+B) : 4 heures

Documents autorisés : aucun

PREMIÈRE PARTIE (A) : SYNTHÈSE DE DOCUMENTS

Contenu du dossier : trois articles et un document iconographique. Les documents sont numérotés 1, 2, 3 et 4.

Sans paraphraser les documents proposés dans le dossier, le candidat réalisera une synthèse de celui-ci, en mettant clairement en valeur ses principaux enseignements et enjeux dans le contexte de l'aire géographique de la langue choisie, et en prenant soin de n'ajouter aucun commentaire personnel à sa composition.

La synthèse proposée devra comprendre entre 600 et 675 mots et sera rédigée intégralement dans la langue choisie. Elle sera en outre obligatoirement précédée d'un titre proposé par le candidat.

SECONDE PARTIE (B) : TEXTE D'OPINION

En réagissant aux arguments exprimés dans cet éditorial (document numéroté 5), le candidat

rédigera lui-même dans la langue choisie un texte d'opinion d'une longueur de 500 à 600 mots.

A - Document 1

Artificial intelligence might be a threat to humans

but not for the reasons you think

By Nigel Shadbolt(1), *The Guardian*, Thursday 22 January 2015

[...] Our computers are getting better thanks to the exponential developments that drive this area of science and engineering. The computer you buy today is obsolete in R&D terms and yet is roughly twice as powerful as the one the same money could buy 18 months earlier. This has been happening for decades.

My students have access to computers that are 1 million times more powerful than the ones I began my AI research on back in the late 1970s. If we had improved air travel as fast I would fly from London to Sydney in less than a tenth of a second.

As well as more powerful computers, we have learned how to write software that "learns" to get better, "understands" human speech, and "navigates" from one place to another. I put the verbs in quotes because for the most part in AI we are not claiming that the algorithms operate in the way that we do when we solve similar tasks.

A founding father of AI once said "there are lots of ways being smart that aren't smart like us". What we have built in AI are numerous slivers of smart behaviour, a digital ecosystem populated with adaptive systems narrowly crafted to a particular niche.

When a high-end computer beat Garry Kasparov, the world chess champion, in the 90s it didn't usher in a new age of intelligent machines. It did demonstrate what you could do with large amounts of computer power, large databases full of moves and good heuristics to look ahead and search possible moves. The overall effect on the world chess champion was unnerving. Kasparov felt as if Deep Blue was reading his mind. Deep Blue had no concept there was another mind involved.

But it is easy to endow our AI systems with general intelligence. If you watch the performance of IBM's Watson as it beats reigning human champions in the popular US TV quiz show you feel you are in the presence of a sharp intelligence. Watson displays superb general knowledge – but it has been exquisitely trained to the rules and tactics of that game and loaded with comprehensive data sources from Shakespeare to the Battle of

Medway. But Watson couldn't play Monopoly. Doubtless it could be trained – but it would be just another specialised skill.

We have no clue how to endow these systems with overarching general intelligence. Deep Mind, a British company acquired by Google, has programs that learn to play old arcade games to superhuman levels. All of this shows what can be achieved with massive computer power, torrents of data and AI learning algorithms. But our programs are not about to become self-aware. They are not about to apply a cold calculus to determine that they and the planet would be better off without us.

What of "emergence" – the idea that at a certain point many AI components together display a collective intelligence – or the concept of "hard take off" a point at which programs become themselves self-improving and ultimately self-aware? I don't believe we have anything like a comprehensive idea of how to build general intelligence – let alone self-aware reflective machines.

But there are lots of ways of being smart that aren't smart like us, and there is the danger that arises from a world full of dull, pedestrian dumb-smart programs. Of hunter kill drones that just do one thing very well – take out human targets. Done at scale this becomes an existential risk. How reflective does a system have to be to wreak havoc. Not at all if we look to nature and the self-replicating machines of biology such as Ebola and HIV.

AI researchers are becoming aware of the perils as well as the benefits of their work. Drones full of AI recognition and target acquisition software alarm many. We need restraints and safeguards built into the heart of these devices. In some cases we might seek to ban their development altogether.

We might also want to question the extent and nature of the great processing and algorithmic power that can be applied to human affairs, from financial trading to surveillance, to managing our critical infrastructure. What are those tasks that we should give over entirely to our machines? These are ethical questions we need to attend to. [...]
(717 words)

---

(1) About the author : Sir Nigel Richard Shadbolt is Principal of Jesus College, Oxford, and Professorial Research Fellow in the Department of Computer Science, University of Oxford. He is Chairman of the Open Data Institute which he co-founded with Sir Tim Berners-Lee. He is also a Visiting Professor in the School of Electronics and Computer Science at the University of Southampton.

A - Document 2

The Master Algorithm : A world remade by machines that learn

By Anil Ananthaswamy, *New Scientist*, October 28, 2015

WHEN machine learning algorithms that replace newspaper reporters became fodder for a recent episode of Comedy Central's The Daily Show, it was clear that the technology had gone mainstream.

But as Pedro Domingos points out in The Master Algorithm, machines that learn have been deeply involved with our lives for a while. If you use Google, Netflix, Amazon, Pandora, Yelp, Xbox or just about any online dating service, your life is being run by algorithms that are learning more and more about you by chomping on the data you, sometimes unwittingly, provide.

"Society is changing, one learning algorithm at a time. Machine learning is remaking science, technology, business, politics and war," writes Domingos, a computer scientist at the University of Washington, Seattle. For people in his field, the problem is that there are myriad such algorithms, each trying to discern patterns in the masses of data we produce. "Machine learning is about prediction," he writes, "predicting what we want, the results of our actions, how to achieve our goals, how the world will change."

The book is about the quest for that one master algorithm which would change machine learning, and hence our lives, irrevocably. If it exists, says Domingos, the master algorithm can derive all knowledge in the world "past, present, and future – from data". In theory, such an algorithm could derive Newton's laws from the astronomical observations of Tycho Brahe, with no a priori knowledge of such laws.

But why should such an algorithm even exist? Domingos provides compelling arguments from neuroscience, evolution, physics, statistics and computer science. For instance, the cerebral cortex might be an instance of such an algorithm : some neuroscientists think that it implements the same algorithm all over, just tweaked to learn to see or hear, or to make sense of touch.

Depending on your world view, the development of a master algorithm is either really thrilling or downright scary. It's not surprising that Domingos, an expert in machine learning, has a very optimistic view. He clearly sees the master algorithm as desirable and maybe even inevitable. This cheery outlook shines through large parts of the book, when he writes that such an algorithm will "speed poverty's decline", that routine jobs "will be automated and replaced by more interesting ones", that the health of our planet will "take a turn for the better", and that our own lives will be "longer, happier and more productive".

Domingos has few doubts, and those he has mainly concern whether the technology will really happen as promised. "Maybe," he muses, "the master algorithm will take its place among the great chimeras, alongside the philosopher's stone and the perpetual motion machine."

But what about the future that lies in store for us, should machine learning take over our lives (if it hasn't already)? Again, Domingos sees it all as a positive. "Someday there'll be a robot in every house, doing the dishes, making the beds, even looking after the children while the parents work. How soon depends on how hard finding the Master Algorithm turns out to be." [...]

It's hard to avoid the feeling that machine learning is only going to increase the rift between the haves and the have-nots, as we enter a new phase of survival of the fittest. As Domingos writes, "He who learns fastest wins", and machine learning "is the latest chapter in the arms race of life on Earth".

But he's still not worried. As machine learning does away with most jobs, the world Domingos envisions consists of a large class of unemployed people living on a permanent basic income doled out by the government, while those in the few remaining human occupations will be stupendously wealthy. "For those of us not working, life will not be meaningless, any more than life on a tropical island where nature's bounty meets all needs is meaningless." [...] (645 words)

The Master Algorithm : How the quest for the ultimate learning machine will remake our world Pedro
Domingos   Basic Books/Penguin

A – Document 3

How We Can Overcome the Risks of AI

Andrew Lohn, Andrew Parasiliti and William Welser IV, *Time Magazine*, October 22, 2015

Apple's recent acquisition of Vocal IQ, an artificial intelligence company that specializes in voice programs, should not on its face lead to much fanfare : It appears to be a smart business move to enhance Siri's capabilities. But it is also another sign of the increased role of AI in our daily lives. While the warnings and promises of AI aren't new, advances in technology make them more pressing. Forbes reported this month: "The vision of talking to your computer like in Star Trek and it fully understanding and executing those commands are about to become reality in the next 5 years." Antoine Blondeau, CEO at Sentient Technologies Holdings, recently told Wired that in five years he expects "massive gains" for human efficiency as a result of artificial intelligence, especially in the fields of health care, finance, logistics and retail.

Blondeau further envisions the rise of "evolutionary intelligence agents," that is, computers which "evolve by themselves – trained to survive and thrive by writing their own code—spawning trillions of computer programs to solve incredibly complex problems."

While Silicon Valley enthusiasts hail the potential gains from artificial intelligence for human efficiency and the social good, Hollywood has hyped its threats. AI-based enemies have been box office draws at least since HAL cut Frank Poole's oxygen hose in *2001 : A Space Odyssey*. And 2015 has truly been the year of fictional AI provocateurs and villains with blockbuster movies including *Terminator Genisys, Ex-Machina, and The Avengers : Age of Ultron*. But are the risks of AI the domain of libertarians and moviemakers, or are there red flags to be seen in the specter of "intelligence agents?" Silicon Valley cannot have "exponential" technological growth and expect only positive outcomes. Similarly, Luddites can't wish away the age of AI, even if it might not be the version we see in the movies.

The pace of AI's development requires an overdue conversation between technology and policy leaders about the ethics, legalities and real life disruptions of handing over our most routine tasks to what we used to just call "machines." But this conversation needs to focus increasingly on near-term risks, not just cinematic ones.

For example, even if a supercomputer's coding is flawless, and someday self-generated, and is protected from being infected by a warring nation-state, a hacktivist, or even an angry teenager, AI can still produce wrong answers. A *Wired* article from January 2015 showed just how wrong. When presented with an image of alternating yellow and black parallel, horizontal lines, state of the art AI saw a school bus and was 99% sure it was right.

How far can we trust AI with such control over the Internet of Things, including our health, financial, and national defense decisions? There is a service to be done in developing a deeper understanding of the reasonable precautions needed to mitigate against coding flaws, attackers, infections and mistakes while enumerating the risks and their likelihoods.

Applied to military systems the risks are obvious, but commercial products designed by AI could produce a wide range of unexpected negative outcomes. One example might be designing fertilizers that help reduce atmospheric carbon. The Environmental Protection Agency tests such products before they are approved so dangerous ones can be discovered before they are released. But if AI only designs products that will pass the tests, is that AI designing inherently safe products or simply ones capable of bypassing the safeguards? [...]

Can the risks posed by AI be completely eliminated? The short answer is no, but they are manageable, and need not be cause for alarm. The best shot at providing adequate safeguards would be regulating the AI itself : requiring the development of testing protocols for the design of AI algorithms, improved cybersecurity protections, and input validation standards—at the very least. Those protections would need to be specifically tailored to each industry or individual application, requiring countless AI experts who understand the technologies, the regulatory environment, and the specific industry or application. At the same time, regulatory proposals should be crafted to avoid stifling development and innovation.

AI needs to enter the public and political discourse with real-world discussion between tech gurus and policymakers about the applications, implications and ethics of artificial intelligence. Specialized AI for product design may be possible today, but answering broad questions such as, "Will this action be harmful?" is well outside the capabilities of AI systems, and probably their designers as well.

Answering such questions might seem like an impossible challenge, but there are signs of hope. First, the risks with AI, as with most technologies, can be managed. But the discussions have to start. And second, unlike in an AI-themed Hollywood thriller, these machines are built to work with humankind, not against it. It will take an army of human AI experts to keep it that way, but precautions can and should be sought now. (812 words)

A – Document 4

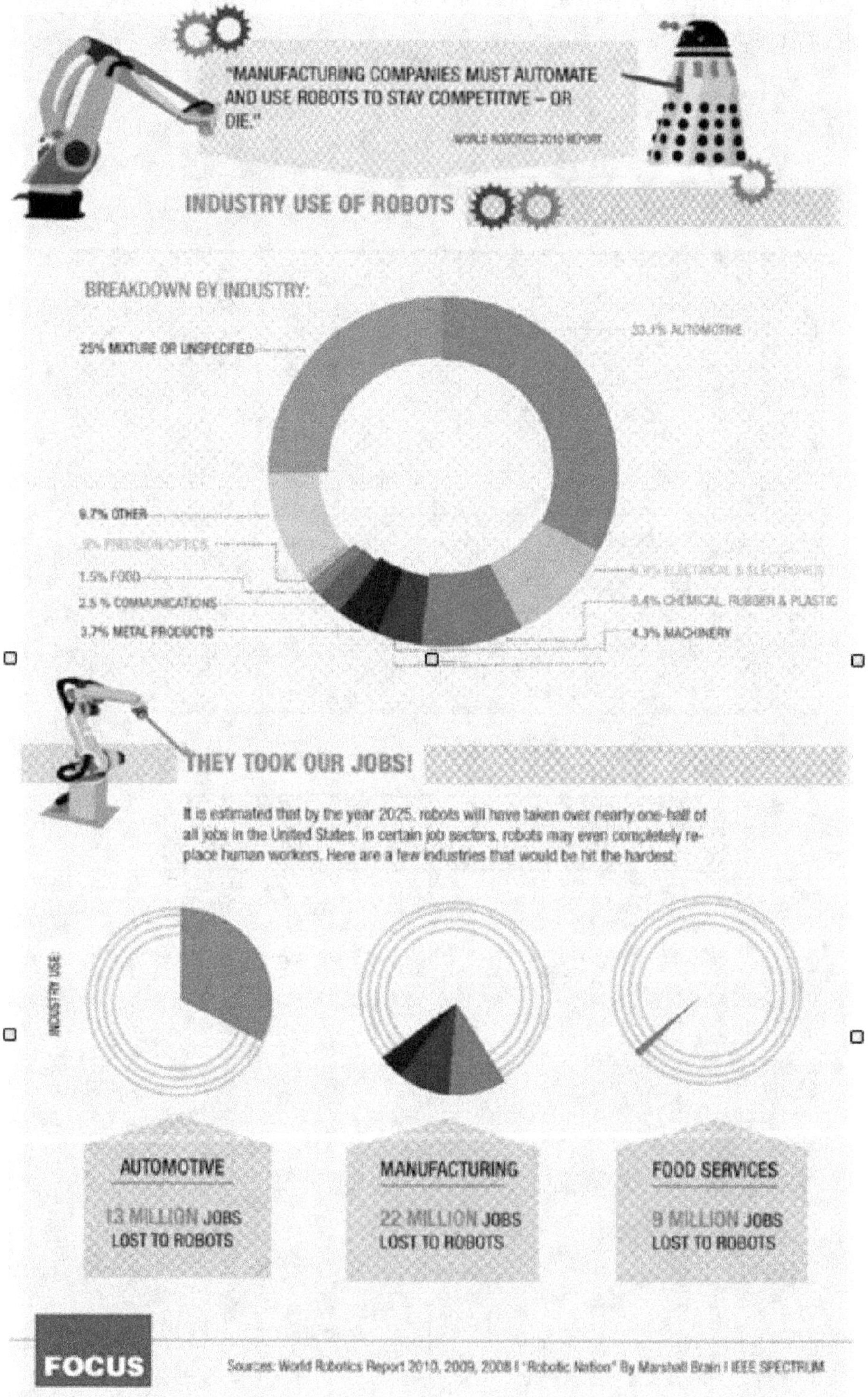
"MANUFACTURING COMPANIES MUST AUTOMATE AND USE ROBOTS TO STAY COMPETITIVE – OR DIE."
WORLD ROBOTICS 2010 REPORT
INDUSTRY USE OF ROBOTS
BREAKDOWN BY INDUSTRY:
25% MIXTURE OR UNSPECIFIED
33.1% AUTOMOTIVE
9.7% OTHER
1.5% FOOD
2.5 % COMMUNICATIONS
3.7% METAL PRODUCTS
6.4% CHEMICAL, RUBBER & PLASTIC
4.3% MACHINERY
THEY TOOK OUR JOBS!
It is estimated that by the year 2025, robots will have taken over nearly one-half of all jobs in the United States. In certain job sectors, robots may even completely replace human workers. Here are a few industries that would be hit the hardest:
INDUSTRY USE:
AUTOMOTIVE
13 MILLION JOBS LOST TO ROBOTS
MANUFACTURING
22 MILLION JOBS LOST TO ROBOTS
FOOD SERVICES
9 MILLION JOBS LOST TO ROBOTS
FOCUS
Sources: World Robotics Report 2010, 2009, 2008 I "Robotic Nation" By Marshall Brain I IEEE SPECTRUM

B - Document 5

Robot Rights Rule! Artificial intelligence challenges the distinction between man and machine

By *The Washington Times*, Sunday, July 26, 2015

The season of the Theater of the Absurd continues. After the Supreme Court twisted the clear meaning of plain English words to save Obamacare and bless same-sex marriage, after Iran hoodwinked Barack Obama into preserving and expanding its nuclear program, after Bruce Jenner remade himself (herself? itself?) into a buxom synthetic female, no one should be surprised when R2D2 wakes up to demand his civil rights, too. This might not be what Mr. Obama had in mind, but a conscientious radical accepts everything new, bad or not.

If self-awareness is the essence of what it means to be human, and humans merit rights, machines may soon be ready to claim their birthright (assembly-right?). Computer scientists at Rensselaer Polytechnic Institute in Troy, N.Y., have taught humanoid robots to recognize themselves as distinct from others. Taking a group of three robots, researchers administered a "dumbing pill" program to two of them, which told them they were unable to speak. When the group was asked which one could still speak, the third robot spoke up, recognized its own voice and announced that it was the one. It's not exactly Descartes, "I think, therefore I am," but for a robot, it's not bad.

Robo-ethics, the morality of how robots are designed and tasked, is challenging scientists and engineers to ponder the possibility – some say the inevitability – of artificial intelligence advancing far beyond simple self-awareness, to outsmart the creators. Once they comprehend the concept of personhood, robots could grasp the idea that society is obligated to grant them rights, similar to the human rights described in the Declaration of Independence, such as "life, liberty and the pursuit of happiness." But will a happy robot be a good robot?

An ethicist says that now is the time to ponder the enigmatic questions of cyber law: "Robotic systems accomplish tasks in ways that cannot be anticipated in advance; and robots increasingly blur the line between person and instrument," says Ryan Calo, a professor at the University of Washington School of Law. If, in the future, a demonstrably sentient machine claims the right that humans have to procreate, or build copies of itself, who can say nay? When the multiplying machines petition for the right of representation in governance, men and women born of nature will face an ethical dilemma. "Which right do we take away from this sentient entity, then," Professor Calo asks, "the fundamental right to copy, or the deep, democratic right to participate?"

Bringing down the curtain on this season of the Theater of the Absurd, by ordaining that rights are reserved for flesh-and-blood humans, may not be that simple. As replacing human hips and knees has become routine medicine in the 21st century, so might integration of bionic body parts to remedy the ravages of injury or disease in coming decades. Should society draw the line between man and machine when cyborgs – part living, part mechanical – show up at the courthouse to register to vote? The befuddlement that accompanied the use of the "one-drop rule" in determining the race of Americans of mixed ancestry in years past, would be minor by comparison.

If robot rights seem a stretch, animal rights sound equally silly, but one nonhuman creature has won rudimentary human rights. In 2014, an orangutan in Argentina named Sandra was granted legal personhood through the imagination of the lawyers. A court ordered Sandra released from prison (a zoo, actually) on the grounds that as an intelligent, nonhuman primate, she is entitled to the freedom to live in a sanctuary rather than in a cage.

Believing that artificial intelligence will soon render robots to be humans of a different kind, one socially insensitive wag has taken up their cause with a slogan : "Robot lives matter." Don't laugh.

(628 words)

CORRIGE SYNTHESE X 2016

The next Frontier for Artificial Intelligence : Artificial Conscience ?

Big data has energized the development of AI with stimulating prospects; however these have come with questioning from the scientific community and the broader society. In his 2015 *Guardian* paper, British academic Sir Shadbolt doubts that AI can be turned from smart to clever and raises the issue of its current uses. In contrast, computer science specialist Domingos' 2015 book reviewed in *The New Scientist* brims with optimism : the master algorithm that can calculate the world may be around the corner, and with it the advent of better times for all. Not everybody agrees, as a collective 2015 article from *Time* underlines : the popular culture's misgivings about machine control of humans are misplaced, but real perils exist if AI is left to its own devices. Besides, the much-feared replacement of humans by machines is no sci-fi nightmare but an ongoing process in many sectors, as the data from pie charts reproduced by activist group Focus from *IEEE spectrum* magazine shows. Can AI be made self-generating ? And above all, if so, what for? An assessment of the recent developments in AI invites a discussion of the next step, i.e machine learning, its forms and limits, from a scientific viewpoint, and beyond, of the human horizon of the AI experiment.

To Shadbolt, the exponential development of AI since the 1970s has been quantitative rather than qualitative : AI is about highly specialized, increasingly interactive, but not versatile machines; Domingos remarks that software which crunches staggering amounts of data to discern individual patterns and predict trends is irresistibly changing our lives; so far this has impacted surveillance and the development of war robotics, a questionable outcome; and the charts confirm that the US automotive and manufacturing industries combined (which back in 2008-10 accounted for about two thirds of the overall use of robots) are projected to lose 35 million jobs to machines by 2025.

Does this mean that machines may take over humans ? All writers agree that the next big leap is for AI to grow and invent itself. Domingos describes this as the « master algorithm » evolving comprehensive knowledge from data, but Shadbolt believes we're nowhere near this, as we can't yet develop artificial transferable skills and conceptual intelligence. Case in point from *Time* : unlike humans a computer has no judgment with which to correct its flawed « perception ». Therefore the fantasies about AI becoming self-aware and controlling humans are not about to materialize, as both Shadbolt and *Time* emphasize. However there are other perils already looming, calling for some serious thinking : what is humans' place in the algorithm(s) ?

In Shadbolt's view, the danger for humanity is not   an evil, all-controlling « master artificial brain » but the myriad machines that are already around, with formidable skills and autonomy, and no moral checks ; besides, we allow cold algorithmic logic increasingly to rule over critical areas of human activity. The *Time* writers echo this concern : a machine will complete its task even if this involves cheating regulations or causing long-term hazards. Ethical concerns and expert anticipation should therefore inform strict coding protocols ; this view is shared by Shadbolt, though it is somehow at odds with the « hard take-off » theory that AI should ideally generate new code and programming on its own. Domingos favours this leap of faith, which would solve the issue of « half of US jobs lost to robots by 2025 » feared by the « luddites » who published the pie charts. The master algorithm would manage the world efficiently, wiping out the donkey work; and the wealth generated could be distributed so that we humans can live richer lives. The view that benefits for humanity are overwhelming is shared by tech CEO Blondeau as quoted in the *Time* piece. But these benefits won't come about without lots of brainwork and caution.

Articial Intelligence is different from ours, but the present and future limits to it undoubtedly depend on our own. (675 words title included)

CORRIGE SUJET B - OPINION - X 2016

Are we about to see robotics impact politics ? This 2015 editorial from the conservative *Washington Times* discusses the implications of transhumanism in order to satirize civil rights claims in the US ; however, in the course of this the writer raises the all-important questions of identity and humanity, the essence of which is being questioned by scientific advances and the blurring of lines between man and machine. He also hints at the *angst* many people feel about a potential power transfer from the former to the latter.

Although the writer of the article uses good science to score political points against US liberals (who, he implies, are ready to grant recognition, rights and compensation to anything that walks on two legs and even four) I think he has a point : the science which makes it possible accurately to identify ethnicity, change one's gender at will, and become in part a cyborg if expedient, is now mainstream or about to be ; but we haven't yet matched it with the necessary in-depth thinking. If nature no longer determines gender, what does ? The same goes for humanity, the essence of which is supposedly conscience. We are human when we think, and realize that we do. The implication is that if machines can be made self-aware, they are human, and therefore entitled to a number of rights.

This fantasy rests on some flawed reasoning. It takes it for granted that conscience, and even consciousness, result from the operations of something akin to a logarithm in the human brain. It applies computer science to neuroscience, rather than the reverse. But what if conscience is not the result of calculus ? Computers are calculating machines, where human intelligence involves affectivity and concept, and also a measure of functional irrationality, and more. Our knowledge of the way our brain works is embryonic and probably as useless as human and social sciences, or even religion, to help create artificial conscience. A computer can probably be made to mimick the operations of a human conscience to answer questions that its programmers will have anticipated, but this will only go as far as their own intelligence does ; the machine will be tricked into showing the limits of its « thinking » by an astute human resorting to paradoxical questions or genuine political obfuscation.

What puzzles me besides is the belief that, should robots become self-aware, they would threaten humans. The writer suggests that granting both reproductive and voting rights to robots would result in them organizing to win power (I suspect this traduces the anxiety of some voter groups in the US facing the demographic shift and the growing clout of minorities.) But even if this happened, there is no logical reason to suppose that robots or transhumans would want to inflict more harm on humans than humans already do on each other. Supposing they would, reveals pessimism about human nature rather than a realistic approach of AI. Machines programmed by man have no reason to turn against him, unless malevolent humans program them to do so. This, indeed, is already happening.

Unfortunately, it is not possible to inscribe sci-fi genius Isaac Asimov's (1) « 3 laws of robotics » into robot brains (« *a robot must never harm a human being, must obey a human being except if this contradicts law n°1, must protect itself except if this involves breaching laws 2 and 3* ») because obeying them ultimately implies a choice between good and bad which is entirely subjective. A machine that would discriminate good from bad with certainty would have to be called God. (600 words)

(1) La Fée Prépa vous conseille de lire au minimum la page wikipédia consacrée à Isaac Asimov, (https://en.wikipedia.org/wiki/Isaac_Asimov) un des plus grands auteurs de science-fiction de tous les temps, dont l'oeuvre explore la thématique de l'intelligence artificielle et les problèmes scientifiques et surtout éthiques et philosophiques qu'elle soulève. Parler d'intelligence artificielle sans évoquer Asimov, c'est un peu comme disserter sur l'histoire de la recherche sur la gravité universelle sans mentionner la loi de Newton. C'est possible, mais ça ne fait pas sérieux.

SUJET CENTRALE-SUPÉLEC 2016

Anglais

MP, PC, PSI

Durée : 4 heures

Calculatrices interdites. L'usage de tout système électronique ou informatique est interdit dans cette épreuve.

Rédiger en anglais et en 500 mots une synthèse des documents proposés, qui devra obligatoirement comporterun titre. Indiquer avec précision, à la fin du travail, le nombre de mots utilisés (titre inclus), un écart de 10% en plus ou en moins sera accepté.

Ce sujet propose les 4 documents suivants :

– la déclaration *Why photograph war?* de James Nachtwey écrite en 1985 ;

– un billet du blog *Media Myth Alert* de W. Joseph Campbell, publié le 20 mai 2014 ;

– un article intitulé Raw, Relevant History de Victor Davis Hanson, paru dans le *New York Times* le 18 avril 1998 ;

– History of the airplane, un poème de Lawrence Ferlinghetti écrit en réaction aux attentats du 11 septembre 2001 aux États-Unis.

L'ordre dans lequel se présentent les documents est aléatoire.

Document 1

Nachtwey's credo

In 1985, shortly before becoming a member of the world famous photo agency Magnum, the then 36-year-old James Nachtwey wrote the following text, a credo about the relevance of his work as a war photographer.

Why photograph war?

There has always been war. War is raging throughout the world at the present moment. And there is little reason to believe that war will cease to exist in the future. As man has become increasingly civilized, his means of destroying his fellow man have become ever more efficient, cruel and devastating.

Is it possible to put an end to a form of human behavior which has existed throughout history by means of photography? The proportions of that notion seem ridiculously out of balance. Yet, that very idea has motivated me.

For me, the strength of photography lies in its ability to evoke a sense of humanity. If war is an attempt to negate humanity, then photography can be perceived as the opposite of war and if it is used well it can be a powerful ingredient in the antidote to war.

In a way, if an individual assumes the risk of placing himself in the middle of a war in order to communicate to the rest of the world what is happening, he is trying to negotiate for peace. Perhaps that is the reason why those in charge of perpetuating a war do not like to have photographers around.

It has occurred to me that if everyone could be there just once to see for themselves what white phosphorous does to the face of a child or what unspeakable pain is caused by the impact of a single bullet or how a jagged piece of shrapnel can rip someone's leg off — if everyone could be there to see for themselves the fear and the grief, just one time, then they would understand that nothing is worth letting things get to the point where that happens to even one person, let alone thousands.

But everyone cannot be there, and that is why photographers go there — to show them, to reach out and grab them and make them stop what they are doing and pay attention to what is going on

— to create pictures powerful enough to overcome the diluting effects of the mass media and shake people out of their indifference — to protest and by the strength of that protest to make others protest.

The worst thing is to feel that as a photographer I am benefiting from someone else's tragedy. This idea hauntsme. It is something I have to reckon with every day because I know that if I ever allow genuine compassion to be overtaken by personal ambition I will have sold my soul. The

stakes are simply too high for me to believe otherwise. (472 words)

James Nachtwey(1)

1 James Nachtwey (March 14, 1948) is an American photojournalist and war photographer. He has been awarded the Overseas PressClub's Robert Capa Gold Medal five times and two World Press Photo awards.

Document 2

Exaggerating the power of 'napalm girl' photo

W. Joseph Campbell(2), *Media Myth Alert(3),* May 29, 2014

'Napalm girl,' 1972 (Nick Ut/AP)

The famous "napalm girl" photograph of June 1972 undeniably ranks among the most profound and disturbing images of the Vietnam War. Its power, though, is often overstated.The photograph, taken by Nick Ut of the Associated Press, showed Vietnamese children terror-stricken by a misdirected napalm attack on their village by the South Vietnamese Air Force. At the center of image was a 9-year-old girl named Kim Phuc, shown screaming and naked as she fled. The photograph, formally titled "The Terror of War," won a Pulitzer Prize in 1973.

In the years since then, a tendency has developed to attribute to the image effects that are far more powerful and decisive than it projected at the time.

For example, the Guardian newspaper in London asserted in a review the other day of anexhibit in France of the imagery of war that Ut's photo "galvanized" American "public opinion and expedited the end of the Vietnam war." Neither claim is accurate. By June 1972, American public opinion had long since turned against the war in Vietnam.Nearly 60 percent of respondents to a Gallup poll conducted early in 1971 had said thatthe United States had made a mistake by sending troops to fight in Vietnam. (Gallup periodically has asked the question since 1965, when just 24 percent of respondents said it was a mistake to have sent troops to Vietnam. By August 1968, a majority of respondents said it had been a mistake.)

Ut's photo can hardly be said to have galvanized opinion against the war: That shift had taken place years before. Nor can it be said that the photo "expedited" the war's end. By June 1972, the war was essentially over for American forces in Vietnam. President Richard Nixon had announced in November 1971 that U.S. ground operations had ended in South Vietnam and by June 1972, nearly all U.S. combat units had been removed from the country.

Compelling though it was, the "napalm girl" photo exerted impact far less profound than is now believed.But so what? Why is it problematic to overstate the image's effects? To do so is to indulge in a central flaw of a media-driven myth — that of media centrism, of exaggerating the power of the journalism, of attributing to news media greater influence than they really wield. To do so also is to misread and distort the historical record. No single photograph turned public opinion against the war in Vietnam or "expedited" its end: The war's duration, its uncertain policy objectives, and its toll in dead and wounded all were far more decisive factors in the outcome of the conflict. "Napalm girl" was an unsettling image, undeniably memorable. But it does not follow that it wielded immeasurable or decisive influence.

It did not. (462)

(2)W. Joseph Campbell is a tenured full professor in the American University School of Communication's Communication Studiesprogram.

(3) The Media Myth Alert blog calls attention to the appearance and publication of media-driven myths — stories about and/or bythe news media that are widely believed and often retold but which, under scrutiny, prove to be apocryphal or wildly exaggerated

Document 3

Raw, Relevant History By Victor Davis Hanson

Published: April 18, 1998

FRESNO, Calif. — "Thucydides, an Athenian, wrote the history of the war between the Peloponnesians and the Athenians." With those words a disgraced Athenian admiral matter-of-factly opens "The History of the Peloponnesian War," his monumental, though unfinished, narrative of the 27-year war (431–404 B.C.) between Athens and Sparta that left the Athenian empire and the entire culture of the Greek city-state in ruins.

Because he had lived through and participated in the events he described, Thucydides had an advantage over later historians, who have had to dig through unreliable records and consult secondary sources. But even as he set down his record of contemporary events, Thucydides was eyeing posterity. His work, he boasted, was "not an essay to win applause of the moment, but a possession for all time."

If his contemporaries failed to appreciate his true genius, perhaps people like ourselves would fathom it two and a half millenniums in the future. And so we do. Studying how a seafaring democratic Athens fought an insular oligarchy like Sparta teaches us a lot about current world crises and the fickleness of public opinion. Thucydides knew nothing about peace studies, conflict resolution theory, God's will or the United Nations, but could declare for all time that people go to war over "honor, fear and self-interest." Period.

Thousands of paperback translations of Thucydides are sold each year, bearing out his extraordinary

boast. But if his book, like other great works, is timeless, it is also very difficult, in places even obscure. [...] Then why read him at all? Yet people do — and in surprising places. I teach classics at the California State University campus in Fresno, in the middle of the agricultural central Valley, home to the wayward Bulldogs basketball team, coached by the much maligned Jerry Tarkanian.There's no reason to think a book by an ancient Greek would interest these students. They are the children of farm workers and the working poor from Tulare, who wait in line for a turn on the university's outmoded computers. They are not privileged, nor well prepared for college.

Their reference points come from television, not ballet, computer camp or prep school. [...] At Stanford, where I did graduate work, Thucydides was an entirely different historian from the one I've come to know in Fresno. [...] His book is the subject of many pages of high-flow jargon in which, for example, Pericles' funeral oration is discussed as a dry rhetorical exercise that reflects subjective, not absolute, "truth."

I prefer the analysis offered by a Fresno State student I taught in night class. "Sure, he might have lied a little," he said. "Who doesn't? And what do you expect? Thucydides with a tape recorder?"

Scholars and graduate students talk grandly of Thucydides "the realist" whose bleak assessment of human nature was a valuable antithesis to romanticism. But this remote, literary language takes us far from the actual Thucydides, a hard-eyed pragmatist whose judgments derive from first-hand experience. As a working mother at Fresno put it, "Thucydides might like Carter better, but he'd want Reagan dealing with the Russians." Another student, an immigrant, agreed: "Be trusting with someone else's life — not mine." Students in Fresno savor Thucydides the disgraced admiral. They soak up the street fighting at Plataea, where the women and slaves "yelled from the houses and threw stones and tiles," and root for the bloodhungry Athenians at the slaughter near Delium, who in their fury "fell into confusion in surrounding the enemy and mistook and killed each other."

"I bet he killed a few himself to write like that," observed one student, tattooed and scarred, in a late evening humanities class. "It gets crazy like that in a free-for-all," another added.

In class when we discussed the slaughter of the Athenians on Sicily, which brought a pathetic end to the greatest generation of the greatest Greek city in its greatest age, one student urged me on: "Check it out. Don't be afraid. Read it to us out aloud." I did: The Peloponnesians also came down and butchered them, especially those in the water, which was thus immediately spoiled, but which they went on drinking just the same, mud and all, bloody as it was, most fighting to have it.

If we're to keep the ideas of Greece alive, we must first rekindle the Hellenic spirit, for the two are inseparable. That spirit, though it may already be lost in the Ivy League, thrives here among students working at Burger King and among night-school returnees, who, once hooked on Thucydides' blood and guts, then "but only then" begin to appreciate the power of his thought.

Students working off their tuition in places like Fresno, Turlock and Bakersfield don't need the university to tell them how unique their own lives are and how richly diverse their past experiences are. Instead they welcome a tough guy like Thucydides who shows how their brutal experiences are universal, even banal, and thus explicable through abstract canons that exist "for all time."

In an age like ours in which setbacks and disappointments are dealt with through therapy rather than accepted as evidence of the tragic nature of our existence, Thucydides' honesty comes as a welcome touch of realism. With him there is no "feeling your pain," no pretense of cheap compassion, and there are no easy apologies for what we are and what we have done. Thucydides offers students of all races and classes the reassurance that we are all more alike than we think. And in so doing, he offers wisdom about the present, but relief from it as well. (933 words)

Victor Davis Hanson, a professor of Greek at California State University, Fresno, is the co-author, with John Heath, of "Who Killed Homer? The Demise of Classical Education and the Recovery of Greek Wisdom."

Document 4

History of the airplane

And the Wright brothers said they thought they had invented

something that could make peace on earth

(if the wrong brothers didn't get hold of it)

when their wonderful flying machine took off at Kitty Hawk (4)

into the kingdom of birds but the parliament of birds was freaked out

by this man-made bird and fled to heaven

And then the famous Spirit of Saint Louis (5) took off eastward and

flew across the Big Pond with Lindy at the controls in his leather

helmet and goggles hoping to sight the doves of peace but he did not

Even though he circled Versailles

And then the famous Yankee Clipper (6) took off in the opposite

direction and flew across the terrific Pacific but the pacific doves

were frighted by this strange amphibious bird and hid in the orient sky

And then the famous Flying Fortress (7) took off bristling with guns

and testosterone to make the world safe for peace and capitalism

but the birds of peace were nowhere to be found before or after Hiroshima

And so then clever men built bigger and faster flying machines and

these great man-made birds with jet plumage flew higher than any

real birds and seemed about to fly into the sun and melt their wings

and like Icarus crash to earth

And the Wright brothers were long forgotten in the high-flying

bombers that now began to visit their blessings on various Third

Worlds all the while claiming they were searching for doves of

peace

And they kept flying and flying until they flew right into the 21st

century and then one fine day a Third World struck back and

stormed the great planes and flew them straight into the beating

heart of Skyscraper America where there were no aviaries and no

parliaments of doves and in a blinding flash America became a part

of the scorched earth of the world

And a wind of ashes blows across the land

And for one long moment in eternity

There is chaos and despair

And buried loves and voices

Cries and whispers

Fill the air

Everywhere

Lawrence Ferlinghetti (8)

Blind Poet, A Tourist of Revolutions (Speaking Out after 9/11)

ed. Maëlstrom, & Le Veilleur, 2004.

(4)Town in North Carolina where the Wright Brothers made the first successful flight in history of a self-propelled aircraft in December 1903.

(5)Airplane in which Charles A. Lindbergh made the first nonstop solo flight from New York to Paris in May 1927.

(6) One of the largest aircraft of the time, the Boeing 314 Clipper was produced between 1938 and 1941. The Yankee Clipper flew across the Atlantic on a route from Southampton to Port Washington, New York. Its inaugural trip occurred on June 24, 1939.

The Clipper fleet was pressed into military service during World War II for ferrying personnel and equipment to the European andPacific fronts.

(7) The Boeing B-17 Flying Fortress, a four-engine heavy bomber aircraft developed in the 1930s for the United States Army Air Corps.

(8) A prominent voice of the wide-open poetry movement that began in the 1950s, Lawrence Ferlinghetti (born in 1919) has writtenpoetry, translation, fiction, theater, art criticism, film narration, and essays. Often concerned with politics and social issues, Ferlinghetti's poetry countered the literary elite's definition of art and the artist's role in the world.

Corrigé Centrale 2016

War as individual narrative and universal experience

In the narratives of history, art and the media, the objective dimension of war is often overlaid by subjective concerns. A case in point is photographer Nachtwey's 1985 credo, an exercise in self-vindication : can one stop war by showing its outrages, as he claims to have attempted? No, says Campbell, who in 2014 debunks the myth of the 'Napalm girl' picture: what stopped the Vietnam war was wariness, not awareness. Most people are not *unaware* of violence, they know it is a part of their own human nature, as Pr Hanson suggests with his experience of underprivileged students relishing Thucydides in 1998. War is a part of us, which spares no one, including the so-called 'peace-makers', Lawrence Ferlinghetti's 2001 poem suggests. Indeed, narrating the war is narrating ourselves, individually and collectively.

Making a living out of showing atrocities is hard on war photographer Nachtwey's conscience, which is why he likes to think his work, especially that showing the collateral damage, leads public opinion to oppose wars; his stance is inspired by the myth of the power of icons on public opinion. This is epitomized by the   shock effect of the 'Napalm girl' picture that supposedly precipitated the end of the Vietnam war ; however, myth buster Campbell dismisses this as rubbish: the Vietnam war died of rational, not emotional causes, being protracted, ill-thought out and costly. Campbell re-establishes the historical truth behind the airy-fairy, self-referential delusions conveyed by the media : when the picture was released, the war was already as good as over.

Not only the tangible horrors of war don't rouse the compassion and pacifism that Nachtwey banks on, but they actually fascinate many, in particular those for whom violence and strife are a part of everyday life. Hanson's unread, unrefined night-class students in the neighborhoods of 'abandoned' America demonstrated an unerring grasp of Thucydides, a far cry form the high-brow, disembodied interpretation favoured by Ivy League academics. The students liked the Greek admiral's no-nonsense approach, his raw depiction of war, 'warts and all', for what it is : a brawl for *honour, fear and self interest*. However, the liberal Hanson is utterly subjective in his narrative, which he uses to settle accounts with the American intellectual establishment. Ferlinghetti is also highly subjective ; his poem is built on a conceit connecting warfare with the history of aviation from the myth of Icarus to 9/11. His piece is, at bottom, a criticism of America's hubris that grew with inventions like the Wrights', and feats like Linbergh's, turning the 'right', wonderful machines into 'wrong' engines of imperialism and destruction. While purportedly 'seeking peace'. To him 9/11 was just retribution, which is a partisan statement.

Nevertheless, even from the subjective documents there emerges a sense of the chronic, unescapable universality of war. The US was eventually caught up with by the history it had created.   Hanson's uneducated 20th Century American students related to Thucydides' subjectivity, which means he achieved his goal of 'making' posterity', ie of becoming universal. And if anything, Nachtwey the award-winning photographer who went to war to make his point, even with the best intentions, and Ferlinghetti's history of US aviation, beautifully illustrate the diachronic universality of the Greek chronicler's point on motives for war. (*546 words title included*)

CONCOURS COMMUNS POLYTECHNIQUES 2016

EPREUVE COMMUNE - FILIERES MP - PC - PSI - TSI - TPC

LANGUE VIVANTE A : ANGLAIS

durée: 3h

L'usage d'un dictionnaire et de machines (calculatrice, traductrice, etc.) est strictement interdit.

Rédiger en anglais et en 400 mots une synthèse des documents proposés, qui devra obligatoirement comporter un titre. Indiquer avec précision, à la fin du travail, le nombre de mots utilisés (titre inclus), un écart de 10 %en plus ou en moins sera accepté.Vous aurez soin d'en faciliter la vérification, soit en précisant le nombre de mots par ligne, soit enmettant un trait vertical tous les vingt mots.Veillez à bien indiquer, en introduction, la source et la date de chaque document. Vous pourrez ensuite, dans le corps de la synthèse, faire référence à ces documents par "document 1", "document 2", etc.

Ce sujet comporte les 4 documents suivants :

- **document 1** - Adapté de l'article de Juggun Kazim, Social Media Addiction, extrait de *The Express Tribune*, 11/05/2015.

- **document 2** - Adapté de l'article de Susmita Baral Social Media Addiction Results In Feelings Of Inadequacy, Study Says extrait de *iDigitalTimes*, 08/12/2015.

- **document 3** - Adapté de l'article de Holly Willard, Clinical Director at James Mason Centers for Recovery, Is Social Media Addictive? extrait de *jmcrecovery.com*, 03/09/2015.

- **document 4** - Graphique extrait du *GlobalWebIndex*, 26/01/2015.

Les documents ont une égale importance.

A - Document 1

Social Media Addiction

Juggun Kazim, The Express Tribune

11/05/2015.

When we think of addicts, the picture that normally comes to mind is that of a gaunt man or woman, huddled in a corner, trying desperately to get his/her next fix of heroin. But addiction isn't just about substance abuse. If a person engages in an activity (gambling, for instance) to the point where it becomes compulsive and interferes with ordinary life, then as per *Psychology Today*, that too counts as addiction. Now look around you. If you are the parent of a teenager, chances are that your child is too busy communing with his or her smartphone to give you the time of day. If you're a young adult, chances are that you live a large part of your life in the virtual world. We tend to take such behaviour as normal. But in an increasing number of cases, such behaviour isn't normal. It has crossed the line over into addiction.

A number of studies have looked at not only internet addiction generally, but addiction to social networking websites, and Facebook in particular. For example, a recent study at the University of Albany found that excessive use of online social networking websites like Facebook can not only be addictive, but that such usage may be associated with problems such as substance abuse.

Similarly, an earlier study at the University of Bergen found that women, extroverts and people unable to sleep until very late at night were particularly in danger of becoming addicted to Facebook. Yet another study by researchers in California found that the compulsive use of social media websites such as Facebook resulted in the same kind of changes in people's brains as those caused by drug addiction.

As in the case of other types of addiction, there are two types of behaviours found in internet addiction. The first is a constant or increasing desire to interact with the object of the addiction. The second is feeling bad when that interaction isn't available.

In the case of social media websites, what hooks people is the rush they get from social recognition, the thrill of getting a 'like' or a re-tweet. That 'social high' causes addictive personalities to check their Facebook, Instagram and Twitter timelines every few minutes. But as soon as they hit one level of social recognition, they want to go one level higher. Suddenly, it's no longer enough to have five friends laugh at your clever turn of phrase or status on Facebook;

it has to be at least 50. And when you hit 50, then it has to be 100. And so it goes.

But what's wrong with all this, you might ask? At the end of the day, nobody gets hurt if somebodyspends too much time on Facebook, Instagram, Snapchat or Twitter.

Unfortunately, people do get hurt – just not visibly. In the obvious sense, a person who is so obsessed with their Facebook status that they have to check it every few minutes is not going to be very productive at work. We all like to think we are masters of multi-tasking. But the truth is that except for a few genetically blessed individuals, the rest of us are terrible at it. And what that means is that every time we leave a Facebook window open on our work computer, we are all but ensuring that very little work will get done, and that too of mediocre quality.

There are other losses as well. Take, for example, the selfie obsession that has taken social media by storm. Unattractive and equally unnecessary, these selfies are taken anywhere and everywhere. The most memorable and shocking would have to be the one taken by a […] girl with a huge grin on her face sitting in front of a dead body at a funeral. It's not just the fact that such behaviour is frightening and highly inappropriate. It's also the fact that the self-esteem of so many people seems to hang on how many 'likes' their selfies get.

I don't want to suggest that we all go back to an age before computers. Yes, Facebook can be great for catching up with your friends and family. Yes, Twitter can be fun and amusing. The only point is that you have to know what you're dealing with. Social media is the equivalent of candy for the brain. Yes, it's good to get a sugar rush once in a while. But if you do nothing but live on chocolate frosted doughnuts, you're not going to be too healthy. (750 words)

Document 2

Social Media Addiction Results In Feelings Of Inadequacy

Susmita Baral, iDigitalTimes

08/12/2015

Social media addicts may seem like they have a great thing going when you look at their shares and posts, but a new study has found otherwise. A survey has disclosed that those who post regularly on Facebook and Instagram have one common goal: to glamorize their life so it looks more interesting than it really is.

While one would think posting attractive selfies and fun-filled holiday photos would help boost a user's spirits, the exact opposite has been observed. In fact, those who use social media regularly are more likely to feel lower about their careers and looks than their counterparts who stay away from social media.

The study – which was conducted by the Future Foundation and surveyed 5,000 Britons – found that people felt worse because they constantly compare themselves to their peers.

"Social media usage has created a culture of comparison among today's young people," said Will Seymour, the research firm's 'brand officer,' to *Daily Mail*. "To be satisfied with one's life is to be complacent - the goal is to be in a permanent state of improvement, always striving for something better. With an online culture of direct comparison, it's no surprise that social media usage has a greater bearing on how much people worry about not achieving their potential than income or even education."

These findings echo those from a previous study from Brunel University London, where it was found that those who posted on Facebook more regularly had low self-esteem and narcissists were more likely to update about their achievements.(258 words)

Document 3

Is Social Media Addictive?

Holly Willard, jmcrecovery.com

03/09/2015

People are inherently social by nature. Connection is vital to our survival (emotional and physical). If we are outside the herd, we are more vulnerable to attacks. Our brains are wired to connect. In his book *Social Intelligence*, Daniel Goleman describes that there are parts of our brain that are only activated by face-to-face contact with others. […]

Sometimes that need for human contact is also expressed through social media. According to Matthew Lieberman, a Harvard graduate who is now a lead researcher on the subject and a professor of psychology, psychiatry, and bio-behavioral studies at UCLA, the brain network being used when checking social media is the same one used when we are taking a break from work. In other words, our brains wiring leads us to seek out other people to relax.

Just looking at pictures of other people causes a great deal of activity in the dorsomedial prefrontal cortex. Activity in this part of the brain increases your ability to accurately perceive others and quickly decide which emotions they might be feeling. As Matthew Lieberman puts it, our brains are always trying to reset themselves to think about other minds. Looking at social media, apparently, actually helps with that process.

What about the very real fear many people (especially parents) have about social media addiction? Experts say it's not that simple. If someone spends a lot of time on social media, that certainly can be categorized as social-media overuse, but throwing in the "addiction" term is more a way to escalate the argument than it is an accurate representation of what is going on.

Addiction has a technical definition and is a very specific diagnosis for a specific problem. According to Mark Fabbri of South University, addiction has a lot to do with compulsion. Someone feels a compulsion to consume something or to act in a particular way to the point where it significantly interferes with the ability just to live. […]

The problem with automatically labeling too much time on social media or the Internet as an addiction is that if we apply the word with too generous a hand, it becomes meaningless. Not every person who engages in addictive behavior is an addict. The behavior changes from overuse to addiction when an individual is not able to function adequately. […]

Social media is young enough that we really don't know exactly the long-lasting effects. What is already clear is that this generation is experiencing a huge shift in the way members communicate. Realistically speaking, people who are digital natives have always had electronic devices around and are more likely to communicate by text message than by phone call or face-to-face interaction.

What that means in turn is the definition of normal behavior has changed, and it is unfair for someone who has barely gotten accustomed to the idea of texting to really understand the role texting plays in the life of his children and grandchildren. (490 words)

Document 4EPREUVE COMMUNE - FILIERES MP - PC - PSI - TSI - TPC

Graphique extrait du *GlobalWebIndex*, 26/01/2015
(GlobalWebIndex is the world's largest market research study on the digital consumer.)

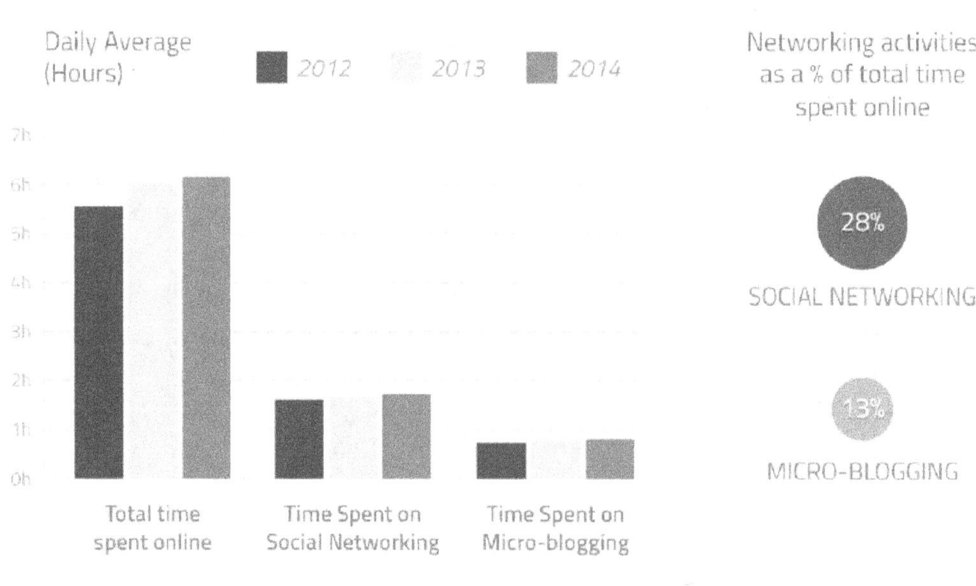

globalwebindex.net /// **Question:** On a typical day, roughly how many hours do you spend on/doing the following? /// **Source:** GlobalWebIndex 2012-2014 (averages across each year) ///
Base: Internet Users aged 16-64

LANGUE VIVANTE B :

ANGLAIS

L'épreuve de langue vivante B est obligatoire pour l'EEIGM Nancy (filières PC et PSI)

Durée: 1h

INSTRUCTIONS GENERALES

Définition et barème :

QCM en trois parties avec quatre propositions de réponse par item.

I. Compréhension : 12 questions (10 points sur 20)

II. Lexique : 12 questions (5 points sur 20)

III. Compétence grammaticale : 15 questions (5 points sur 20)

Réponse juste : + 3

Pas de réponse : 0

Réponse fausse ou réponses multiples : -1

Instructions :

Lisez le texte et répondez ensuite aux questions.

Choisissez parmi les quatre propositions de réponse (A, B, C ou D) celle qui vous paraît la mieux adaptée. Il n'y a qu'une seule réponse possible pour chaque item. (NB: *La Fée Prépa vous conseille de photocopier ce QCM pour entourer les réponses sans abîmer vos précieuses annales*)

Sujet B – Epreuve de QCM - CCP 2016

China's education gap

Every September, the campuses of Peking and Tsinghua Universities, often called the Harvard and M.I.T. of China, <u>brim with</u> eager new students, the winners of China's cutthroat education system. These young men and women possess the outlook of cosmopolitan youth worldwide: sporting designer clothes and <u>wielding</u> high-end smartphones, they share experiences of foreign travel and bond over common fondness for Western television shows like "The Big Bang Theory" and "Sherlock."

They are destined for bright futures. In a few decades, they will fill high-powered positions in government and become executives in state banks and multinational companies. But their ever expanding career possibilities belie the increasingly narrow slice of society they represent. The percentage of students at Peking University from rural origins, for example, has fallen to about 10 percent in the past decade, down from around 30 percent in the 1990s. An admissions officer at Tsinghua University told a reporter last year that the typical undergraduate was "someone who grew up in cities, whose parents are civil servants and teachers, go on family trips at least once a year, and have studied abroad in high school."

China's state education system, which offers nine years of compulsory schooling and admits students to colleges strictly through exam scores, is often <u>hailed</u> abroad as a paradigm for educational equity. The impression is reinforced by Chinese students' consistently <u>stellar</u> performance in international standardized tests. But this reputation is built on a myth. While China has phenomenally expanded basic education for its people, quadrupling its output of college graduates in the past decade, it has also created a system that discriminates against its less wealthy and well-connected citizens, <u>thwarting</u> social mobility at every step with bureaucratic and financial barriers.

A huge gap in educational opportunities between students from rural areas and those from cities is one of the main culprits. Some 60 million students in rural schools are "left-behind" children, cared for by their grandparents as their parents seek work in faraway cities. While many of their urban peers attend schools equipped with <u>state-of-the-art</u> facilities and well-trained teachers, rural students often huddle in decrepit school buildings and struggle to grasp advanced subjects such as English and chemistry amid a <u>dearth</u> of qualified instructors.

For migrant children who follow their parents to cities, the opportunity for a decent education is similarly limited, as various government policies <u>foil</u> their attempts at full integration. The hukou system – a residency status that ties access to <u>subsidized</u> social services to one's hometown – denies rural children the right to enter urban public schools. Many migrant children are relegated to private schools that charge higher tuition and offer <u>subpar</u> education. Recent reforms in cities like Guangzhou and Shanghai have had only a tangential impact on leveling the playing field.

35   In Beijing, home to eight million migrant workers, preconditions for admission seem intended less to promote educational equity than to exacerbate the discrimination. Some parents have switched jobs, <u>sued</u> the government and even engineered divorces to get around onerous documentation requirements, which often vary from district to district. Many urban migrants ultimately have no choice but to send their children back to their rural hometowns for inferior

40   schooling.

China requires a vast majority of students to take the national college entrance examination in

their home province, and elite universities allocate higher admission quotas to first-tier cities like Beijing and Shanghai. One researcher showed that an applicant from Beijing was 41 times more likely to be admitted to Peking University than a comparable student from the poor and largely

45   rural province of Anhui.

Even an urban residency status doesn't ensure educational equity among city dwellers. The quality of urban schools varies widely, and the competition to enter top schools has spawned rampant corruption. Parents fork out tens of thousands of dollars under the guise of "voluntary donations" to secure a slot for their children in elite schools. At top-ranked high schools, such as

50   the one I attended in Beijing, these charges can reach $130,000. Further advantage can be purchased by parents who can pay handsomely to hire teachers to offer extra tutoring to their children, a practice discouraged by the authorities but widespread in reality.

To curb the culture of <u>graft</u>, Beijing has implemented policies this year that require students to attend elementary schools in their home districts. But the new rules, instead of stopping parents

55   from gaming the system, simply channeled the cash to another market. Property in well-regarded school districts became Beijing's hottest commodity this spring. Families have been tripping over one another to trade spacious homes in posh compounds for dilapidated flats next to prestigious elementary schools.(768)

Adapted from The New York Times, September 2014

Sujet B – QCM – CCP 2016

I. COMPREHENSION

Choisissez la réponse qui vous paraît la plus adéquate en fonction du sens du texte.

1. From line 1 to line 6 (paragraph 1), it should be understood that Chinese students:

(A) have a quite different profile from western students.

(B) are luckier than western students.

(C) are not keen on technology.

(D) resemble western students on many points.

2. From line 7 to line 14 (paragraph 2), it should be understood that:

(A) The students graduating from Peking and Tsinghua Universities will be offered top jobs.

(B) Only the brightest of those students will find a job in the future.

(C) Most of those students will work in multinational businesses.

(D) They will be offered more jobs by National banks than multinational firms.

3. From line 7 to line 14 (paragraph 2), it should be understood that, at Peking University:

(A) there are more students than before coming from rural areas.

(B) there are 10% fewer students coming from rural areas, compared with a decade ago.

(C) there are 30% more students coming from rural zones compared with the 1990s.

(D) there were only 10% of students coming from rural areas in the past ten years.

4. From line 15 to line 22 (paragraph 3), it should be understood that the Chinese education system:

(A) is not well considered abroad.

(B) enjoys a good image overseas.

(C) is often criticized by foreign countries.

(D) is seen as being unfair from abroad.

5. From line 15 to line 22 (paragraph 3), it should be understood that:

(A) China has made little effort to promote basic education among the lower classes.

(B) Today fewer and fewer underprivileged Chinese children have access to basic education.

(C) The Chinese government does not make it easy for all to access higher education.

(D) There is no link between social background and access to higher education in China.

6. From line 23 to line 28 (paragraph 4), it should be understood that:

(A) Rural and urban students have the same working conditions.

(B) There are more and more well-trained teachers in rural zones.

(C) Rural schools are as well-equipped as urban ones.

(D) The working conditions in rural schools need to be improved.

7. From line 29 to line 34, it should be understood that:

(A) Because of the hukou system, students from rural areas cannot have access to urban public schools.

(B) The government is trying to bridge the gap between rural and urban schools.

(C) Rural students are easily integrated into public urban schools.

(D) Rural students prefer to integrate private urban schools.

8. From line 29 to line 34 (paragraph 5), it should be understood that:

(A) Only rich students are sent to private schools.

(B) Private schools offer better education than public schools.

(C) Private schools are affordable.

(D) Many underprivileged students have no other choice than joining private schools.

9. From line 35 to line 40 (paragraph 6), it should be understood that in Beijing:

(A) things are made easier for parents to complain about discrimination.

(B) there are more and more students coming from rural areas.

(C) sometimes parents live and work in the city while their children study in rural schools.

(D) many rural families who have moved into the city have ensured their children urban education.

10. From line 41 to 45 (paragraph 7), it should be understood that:

(A) Any Chinese student can join elite universities provided they pass a national entrance examination.

(B) 41% of Beijing's students come from wealthy families.

(C) Joining elite universities is easier when you come from an urban area.

(D) Beijing and Shanghai have set up fair university admission quotas.

11. From line 46 to line 52 (paragraph 8), it should be understood that:

(A) Because of corruption, the quality of urban teaching has decreased.

(B) The authorities encourage parents to offer their children extra-school lessons.

(C) Top schools often impose higher tuition fees.

(D) The government prevents schools from requiring too high tuition fees.

12. From line 53 to line 58 (paragraph 9), it should be understood that:

(A) All elementary schools offer the same teaching quality.

(B) Some families have to make sacrifices to send their children to the best elementary schools.

(C) The access to elementary schools undergoes no government restriction.

(D) Prestigious elementary schools are located next to the rich neighborhoods.

II. LEXIQUE

Choisissez la réponse qui vous paraît la plus appropriée en fonction du contexte.

(les mots sont soulignés dans le texte)

13. brim with (line 2) means:

(A) look for

(B) expect

(C) are full of

(D) welcome

14. wielding (line 4) means:

(A) manipulating

(B) buying

(C) showing

(D) asking for

15. hailed (line 16) means:

(A) praised

(B) called

(C) criticized

(D) copied

16. stellar (line 17) means:

(A) regular

(B) virtual

(C) satisfactory

(D) extraordinary

17. thwarting (line 21) means:

(A) increasing

(B) preventing from happening

(C) pushing

(D) changing

18. state-of-the-art (line 26) means:

(A) artistic

(B) ultramodern

(C) well-designed

(D) national

19. dearth (line 28) means:

(A) number

(B) series

(C) lack

(D) selection

20. foil (line 30) means:

(A) don't show

(B) prove

(C) block

(D) claim

21. subsidized (line 31) means:

(A) unreformed

(B) underprivileged

(C) supported by the government

(D) reduced

22. subpar (line 33) means:

(A) excellent

(B) similar

(C) adapted

(D) below average

23. sued (line 37) means:

(A) approved of

(B) made a legal complaint against

(C) written to

(D) followed

24. graft (line 53) means:

(A) injustice

(B) corruption

(C) discrimination

(D) excellence

III. COMPETENCE GRAMMATICALE

Choisissez la réponse adéquate.

25.

(A) It is all the more difficult as they are poor.

(B) It is all more difficult as they are poor.

(C) It is as more difficult as they are poor.

(D) It is all the more difficult than they are poor.

26.

(A) Many a parent disagree with this policy.

(B) Many a parent disagrees with this policy.

(C) Many parent disagrees with this policy.

(D) Many parents disagrees with this policy.

27.

(A) More the school is prestigious, more the tuition fees are high.

(B) The more prestigious the school, the higher the tuition fees.

(C) More prestigious the school is, higher are the fees.

(D) The more the school is prestigious, the more the tuition fees are high.

28.

(A) They had better to comply with the law.

(B) They had to better comply with the law.

(C) They had better comply with the law.

(D) They had better complying with the law.

29.

(A) It is said wealthy students to be luckier.

(B) It is told wealthy students to be luckier.

(C) Wealthy students are said to be luckier.

(D) Wealthy students are said being luckier.

30.

(A) Had they warned the parents, the latter would have reacted.

(B) If they warned the parents, the latter would have react.

(C) Have they warned the parents, the latter would react.

(D) Had they warned the parents, the latter will react.

31.

(A) If they were richer, they could afford it.

(B) If they have been richer, they could afford it.

(C) If they had been richer, they could afford it.

(D) If they are richer, they could afforded it.

32.

(A) There are less and less students here.

(B) There are less and less of students here.

(C) There are a fewer and fewer students here.

(D) There are fewer and fewer students here.

33. There .... in this university.

(A) are more than 10,000 student

(B) are more 10,000 students

(C) is more 10,000 students

(D) are more than 10,000 students

34. .... they cannot join this school.

(A) Though that they have good results,

(B) Though if they have good results,

(C) Even though they have good results,

(D) If though they have good results,

35. They spent .... on the project.

(A) ten thousands dollars

(B) ten thousand of dollars

(C) ten thousand dollars

(D) ten thousand dollar

36. The authorities offered no other alternative ....

(A) in spite the parents' insistence.

(B) despite of the parents' insistence.

(C) in despite the parents' insistence.

(D) in spite of the parents' insistence.

37. They .... their policy a decade ago.

(A) have reviewed

(B) have review

(C) had review

(D) reviewed

38. The government .... on equity.

(A) should have focused

(B) should to have focused

(C) should have focuse

(D) should have focusing

39. Entrance examinations are becoming ....

(A) the harder and the harder.

(B) more and more hard.

(C) harder and harder.

(D) the more and more harder.

Corrigé Concours Communs Polytechniques 2016 : Synthèse

Social media : an addiction with a twist ?

Does social media compound our bad habits and troubles , or does it only signal a generational behavioral change ? Opinions are divided, witness this set of documents: a May 2015 *Express Tribune* op-ed by J. Kazim expresses alarm at the similarity between social media use and addiction to substances. Besides, they supposedly generate low self-esteem, according to the *Digital Times* in December 2015. However, not everybody agrees: *jmcrecovery* in September 2015 explains that overuse is not necessarily addiction ; it could just be a sign of the times, as the chart showing social media use and micro-blogging use confirms.

According to Kazim, many studies converge to show that social media use is akin to addiction in the way it fosters compulsive behaviour, triggers withdrawal symptoms, and requires increasing doses of approval, the way heroin addicts need more and more of the substance to function. This seems to be borne out by the chart, which shows a steady growth of the use of social media and micro blogging between 2012 and 2014. But then, this growth is inscribed in the overall growth of internet use, and the proportion of social media use to internet use remains stable. Furthermore, the addiction theory is challenged by the author of the *jmcrecovery* op-ed : social media activity is not substantially different from the rest of our 'real' socialization activities. It stimulates the same brain zones as when we interact with real people. It teaches us to accommodate their thinking and emotions.

Besides, the same piece warns, there is a generational phenomenon. Millenials use internet more than older people, and therefore use social media more. Does this mean they are acting 'abnormally ' ? Maybe norms should be redefined. Of course, there are downsides, as the *Digital Times* underlines. People who have issues with self-esteem and ego tend to use social media as a palliative, and it backfires. People who constantly check Facebook at work may have productivity issues, Kazim rightly points out. (338 words)

Corrigé Concours Communs Polytechniques 2016 SUJET B : QCM

Rappel du barème :

Bonne réponse= +3

mauvaise réponse= -1

pas de réponse ou réponses multiples = 0

Pour calculer votre note finale de QCM sur 20 vous devez donc diviser votre total de points de COMPREHENSION par 3,6, celui de LEXIQUE par 7,2 et celui de COMPETENCE GRAMMATICALE par 9, puis faire la somme de ces trois résultats.

I. COMPREHENSION (*12 questions = 10 points*)

1. *(D) resemble western students on many points.*

2. *(A) The students graduating from Peking and Tsinghua Universities will be offered top jobs.*

3. *(D) there were only 10% of students coming from rural areas in the past ten years.*

4. *(B) enjoys a good image overseas.*

5. *(C) The Chinese government does not make it easy for all to access higher education.*

6. *(D) The working conditions in rural schools need to be improved.*

7. *(A) Because of the hukou system, students from rural areas cannot have access to urban public schools.*

8. *(D) Many underprivileged students have no other choice than joining private schools.*

9. *(C) sometimes parents live and work in the city while their children study in rural schools.*

10. *Joining elite universities is easier when you come from an urban area.*

11. *(C) Top schools often impose higher tuition fees.*

12. *(B) Some families have to make sacrifices to send their children to the best elementary schools.*

II. LEXIQUE *(12 questions = 5 points)*

13. brim with (line 2) means:

(C) are full of

14. wielding (line 4) means:

(C) showing

15. hailed (line 16) means:

(A) praised

16. stellar (line 17) means:

(D) extraordinary

17. thwarting (line 21) means:

(B) preventing from happening

18. state-of-the-art (line 26) means:

(B) ultramodern

19. dearth (line 28) means:

(C) lack

20. foil (line 30) means:

(C) block

21. subsidized (line 31) means:

(C) supported by the government

22. subpar (line 33) means:

(D) below average

23. sued (line 37) means:

(B) made a legal complaint against

24. graft (line 53) means:

(B) corruption

III. COMPETENCE GRAMMATICALE *(15 questions = 5 points)*

25. *(A) It is all the more difficult as they are poor.*

26. *(B) Many a parent disagrees with this policy.*

27. *(B) The more prestigious the school, the higher the tuition fees.*

28. *(C) They had better comply with the law.*

29. *(C) Wealthy students are said to be luckier.*

30. *(A) Had they warned the parents, the latter would have reacted.*

31. *(A) If they were richer, they could afford it.*

32. *(D) There are fewer and fewer students here.*

33. There .... in this university.

(D) are more than 10,000 students

34. .... they cannot join this school.

(C) Even though they have good results,

35. They spent .... on the project.

(C) ten thousand dollars

36. The authorities offered no other alternative ....

(D) in spite of the parents' insistence.

37. They .... their policy a decade ago.

(D) reviewed

38. The government .... on equity.

(A) should have focused

39. Entrance examinations are becoming ....

(C) harder and harder.

CONCOURS ARTS ET MÉTIERS ParisTech - ESTP – POLYTECH (e3a)

Épreuve de Langue Vivante MP - PC - PSI

Durée : 3 h

Pour cette épreuve, l'usage des machines (calculatrices, traductrices,…) et de dictionnaires est interdit.

Vous rédigerez en anglais et en 400 mots une synthèse des documents proposés. Vous indiquerez avec précision à la fin de votre synthèse le nombre de mots qu'elle comporte. Un écart de 10% en plus ou en moins sera accepté. Votre synthèse comportera un titre comptabilisé dans le nombre de mots.

Document 1

UK gender gap continues to widen

The UK has slipped out of the top 20 countries for gender equality and the gap between men and women in the workplace has widened, according to a report that places Britain behind the Scandinavian countries and the Philippines. Research by the World Economic Forum (WEF) […] found the UK has slipped from 18th to 26th in the rankings of its Global Gender Gap Report, part of a steady decline from the forum's inaugural league table in 2006, when the UK was ranked ninth.

[…] While the UK failed to make the top 20 in any of the report's four categories – economy, education, health and politics – the drop in its overall rating this year was chiefly attributable to a significantly lower score in "economic participation," which measures attributes such as the ratios of women in the workforce, wage equality for similar work done by men, and the number of womenin senior roles.

[…] The WEF report is the latest in a line of studies and campaigns seeking to highlight gender inequality issues. Last week a global study of almost 6,000 MBA graduates by research group Catalyst found that the most highly qualified female business graduates lack the ambition of male counterparts in sectors such as engineering, manufacturing and natural resources. That finding appeared to be supported by comments from Moya Greene, chief executive of Royal Mail and one of only five female chief executives in the FTSE 100. In a speech last week, she said: "It's still disappointing when you see how young women view their ambition – and how others view that ambition." […] In 2011 the UK government launched a review of women on boards by Lord Davies, which set a target of having a minimum of 25% female representation on FTSE 100 boards by 2015. […] The latest figures show that 61 members of the FTSE 100 have yet to reach 25%.

[…] Ruth Sealy, a lecturer and researcher in organisational psychology at City University London, said: "One of the approaches beginning to have an effect is this continual push for transparency in reporting. It is beginning to have an impact as it makes organisations a lot more aware about what's going on internally and a bit more embarrassed about it. We are not in the same place we were five years ago. The whole women on boards thing has had an impact. It is finally beginning to have an impact on chief executives." (416 words)

Adapted from Simon Goodley, *The Guardian*, 28 Oct 2014

Document 2

If you're a man, is it better to have a male or female boss?

Gallup has been asking Americans whether they'd prefer a male or female boss since the early 1950s and, while the trends are in the direction of equality, overall, both sexes still say they'd prefer a man. What is perhaps most striking is that women plump for male bosses more strongly than men: in 2014, 39 per cent of women said they'd prefer a male boss, against only 26 per cent of men.

Moreover, far more men say there's no difference. So, case closed, right? Even women say men are better bosses. Well, no. For starters women have centuries of male-dominated history counting against them. Even now, in the UK, only 35 per cent of managers are female. So, people are twice as likely to have had a male manager than a female manager – and the higher you go and the older you get, the more pronounced this bias gets. Thus, for many people this kind of preference may simply be a case of better the devil you know than the she-devil you don't.

[…] The trouble is, while generalisations about populations are interesting, they're well known to be a very poor guide to individuals. Besides, whatever you might prefer, you very rarely get to choose your boss anyway, so the best, if rather obvious, advice is to recognise your boss as an individual. "Rather than categorising according to stereotypes, the real world challenge is finding a way to work with the boss you have regardless of gender," says Emily Frohlich, client director of business psychologists Nicholson McBride. "You need to have the self-awareness to set aside your perceptions of differences and ask, 'What is this person in front of me like?"

However, to end on a note of positive discrimination, if you are a man who works in a female dominated environment, you are unlikely to be held back: in fact, quite the reverse. Research suggests that, instead of hitting a glass ceiling, you will experience a "glass escalator" and advance more quickly.(334)

Adapted from Rhymer Rigby, *The Telegraph*, 19 Feb 2015

Document 3

At this rate, it'll take 100 years to get gender equality at work

Things are improving so slowly for women in corporate America that we aren't going to achieve gender equality at the top for another 100 years, according to a report released on Wednesday. It's not for the reasons you might think - i.e., it's not a "mommy issue." Both women and men reported feeling strained by the competing pulls of work and family, according to the survey of nearly 30,000 workers at 118 North American companies. The survey was conducted by McKinsey & Company and LeanIn.org, a nonprofit focused on women's advancement founded by Sheryl Sandberg, chief operating officer at Facebook.

The big, ugly, hard-to-fix issue, the study suggests, is gender bias. That contradicts a lot of the conventional wisdom about why women don't make it to the so-called C-suite - the highest levels of a company where you find the jobs with "chief" in the title […]. "Some of the biggest barriers are cultural and related to unconscious biases that impact company hiring, promotion, and development processes," said Dominic Barton, global managing director of McKinsey & Company[…]. A lot of people, for example, believe on some level that women are less competent than men. There's also something called a "maternal bias," in which mothers who do well at their job are disliked - and kept from advancing - because they're believed to be terrible parents.

Women hold 45 percent of entry-level jobs at the companies surveyed, and their ranks thin out as you go higher. Only 27 percent of vice presidents at those companies are women, as are 23 percent of senior vice presidents and 17 percent of C-suite execs. These figures are a very slight improvement from 2012 […]. Very slight - that's where that 100-year estimate comes from.

So what's going on? First off, women aren't quitting their jobs or "opting out." In fact, the survey found that women, on average, quit their jobs at the same rates as men, or even less often. At the higher levels, women are more likely than men to stick around, the study found. The issue is that women aren't getting promoted at the same rate as men - and at every step along the corporate ladder, women say they are less interested in becoming a top executive.

The reasons why are telling. For single women, the main reason they said they didn't want to advance any higher at work was stress. And while women with children said the main reason they didn't want to advance was because of work and family pressures, stress came in at a very close second for that group. […] For men with children, the difficulty of balancing work and family was also the top reason they weren't interested in holding a higher-ranking job - 62 percent of men with children said that, compared to 65 percent of women with children. And mothers were 15 percent more interested in becoming a top executive than the women surveyed who didn't have children.

"Historically, we thought women were less interested in promotions because of their concerns with family responsibilities," Rachel Thomas, the president and co-founder of LeanIn, told The Huffington Post. "This study points to a new reason: […] women say stress and pressure is a top obstacle for them - all women, not just mothers." The stress, Thomas suggests, comes from the bigger hurdles women face at the office. For example, there's research showing that women are often believed to be less competent at their jobs than they really are, while men are often believed to be more competent than they are. Women have to prove themselves again and again.

There's also a Catch-22 involving personality: women who are seen as competent are less likely to be seen as likable, and women viewed as more likable are less likely to be seen as competent, research has shown. "We always say that women walk on a tightrope," Thomas said. "Men are noton that tightrope."(658 words)

Adapted from Emily Peck, *The Huffington Post*, 30 Sept 2015

Document 4

Gender equality: prospects for further transformation

In certain important ways men potentially have much to gain from deeper and more robust forms of gender equality in American life. In a world of real gender equality men would have a richer array of life choices around parenting and work. The dominant models of masculinity make it difficult for many men to play a full and active role in caregiving activities within the family. It is very difficult for men to interrupt their careers to take care of small children. The dominant models of masculinity also promote intense forms of competitiveness that make many men miserable, working excessively long hours, losing sight of more important things in their lives. Further advances towards gender equality will potentially involve a significant restructuring of the rules that govern the relationship between work and family, and this would give both men and women greater flexibility and balance in their lives.

The inequalities in the gender division of labor […] have an impact far beyond simply the specific problem of free time available to men and women within families. It also deeply affects inequalities in the labor market and employment. The greater domestic burdens that, on average, married women have compared to married men act as a significant constraint on the kinds of jobs they can seek in the labor market. It also affects the attitudes of all employers towards prospective women employees. […] If we are to move towards a more equal sharing of the time burdens of family life, this will have to occur through indirect means which change the incentives men and women have around these tasks and, perhaps, affect the balance of power of men and women within these domestic relations as they negotiate over domestic responsibilities. Three policies are particularly relevant here: pay equity; high quality publicly provided childcare services; egalitarian paid parental leave.(306 words)

Adapted from E.0. Wright & J.Rogers, <u>American Society: How It Actually Works</u>, W.W. Norton, 2010

CONCOURS ARTS ET METIERS ParisTech – ESTP – POLYTECH (e3a)

QCM – ANGLAIS FACULTATIF – MP – PC – PSI

Durée : 1h

<u>Définition et barème :</u>

QCM en trois parties avec quatre propositions de réponse par item.

I. Compréhension : 12 questions (10 points sur 20)

II. Lexique : 12 questions (5 points sur 20)

III.Compétence grammaticale : 15 questions (5 points sur 20)

Réponse juste : + 3

Pas de réponse : 0

Réponse fausse ou réponses multiples : - 1

Instructions :

Lisez le texte et répondez ensuite aux questions. Choisissez parmi les quatre propositions de réponse (A, B, C ou D) celle qui vous paraît la mieux adaptée. Il n'y a qu'une seule réponse possible pour chaque item. Reportez votre choix sur la feuille de réponse.

ARTS ET METIERS – ParisTech – ENST – POLYTECH
QCM Facultatif

Are we liberated by tech – or does it enslave us ?

Technology is unruly. New innovations bring with them a host of unintended consequences, ranging from the troubling to the <u>downright</u> depressing. Social media makes us lonely. Too much screen-time makes teenagers fall behind their peers. And at the more feeble end of the spectrum, many of us have walked into an obstacle while texting. Whatever glorious vision animates the
5   <u>moguls</u> of Silicon Valley, it surely can't be this.

We're much better at designing complex systems than we are at predicting their behaviour, argues the writer Edward Tenner. Even though unintended consequences are inevitable, Tenner thinks they can be powerful catalysts for progress. But even the notion of an "intended consequence" is problematic when it comes to tech. Evgeny Morazov points out that we tend to
10   confuse the positive consequences of information technology with intended ones, <u>downplaying</u> the significance of other natural, but rather less noble, <u>upshots</u> like pornography, surveillance and authoritarian control.

Free time is a case in point. Technology makes us more productive, but it's also accused of unreasonably extending the domain of work. So does tech liberate us, or enslave us? And what
15   does it really "intend" to do? In 1930, the economist John Maynard Keynes predicted that the most pressing concern of the man of the future would be "how to occupy the leisure which science and compound interest will have won for him." It hasn't quite turned out that way – but Keynes wasn't entirely off the mark. When we consider the lot of the average labourer of the past, our complaints about work-life balance start to sound pretty <u>peevish</u>. And the rise of
20   technology really has, it seems, given us more free time than ever. So why do we still feel <u>harried</u>?

It's worth noting that modern leisure is just as tech-saturated as work. Americans who subscribe to Netflix spend more time on the site than they do eating and having sex combined, TDG research found. The average Briton spends 1 hour 20 minutes every day monitoring four social
25   media accounts, according to research from the Global Web Index. But all this screen-time makes us uneasy. To co-opt David Foster Wallace's description of attitudes to television in the 1990s, there's a "weird hate-need-fear-6-hrs-daily gestalt" about the whole thing. But technology doesn't just offer us escape. It promises to transfigure our bodies, our minds and our very souls by making us fitter, happier, and more productive - but it does it by insinuating that we're, well, a
30   bit <u>suboptimal</u> as we are. "There's an app for that" comes with a whispered aside: "You know you're doing it wrong, right?"

Criticisms of tech can sound shrill, but it's not antediluvian to notice the impossible desires technology <u>breeds</u>. Our devices present us with simulacra of beautiful, fit, fulfilled people pursuing their dreams and falling in love, and none of them are browsing the web at 11pm on a
35   Saturday night - unlike us. We click and swipe our <u>woebegone</u> way through a vibrant world where nobody who is anybody spends their free time in front of a glowing screen, painfully aware that our only access to that world is through that very glowing screen. But we're no fools. We know that nothing on the web is as it seems. We long to detach ourselves from the whole circus once and for all - and so we turn once again to the internet to research digital detoxes and
40   vent our tech-related spleen. The web has a way of dancing around us, knowingly and self-referentially and maddeningly <u>deflecting</u> every attempt we make to express our unease.

But <u>prying</u> our free time <u>from</u> the clutches of technology isn't necessarily the answer. The German philosopher Theodor Adorno argued that "free time" is an artificial concept – and it's anything but free. For Adorno, free time is the very prorogation of work: it is "nothing more than
45   a shadowy continuation of labour". Today's tech-saturated leisure trade – to say nothing of the trillion-dollar <u>behemoth</u> that is the "wellness industry" – is an integral part of a world in which we are treated as consumers first and citizens second. Talk of reclaiming free time is missing the point. What we need is control of the time we already have. [...] We love to praise tech, and we love to condemn it. We equate it with chaos, power, love, hate; with democracy, with tyranny,
50   with progress and regress - we laud it as our salvation, while lamenting it as our scourge. Like any technology that has come before it, digital technology is all of these things. But it's essentially none of them.

Adapted from The Guardian, December 9, 2015

I. COMPRÉHENSION

Choisissez la réponse qui vous paraît la plus adéquate en fonction du sens du texte.

1. From line 1 to line 5, it should be understood that technology:

(A) has affected adults more than teenagers.

(B) has improved our lives.

(C) has helped fight against loneliness.

(D) has caused great damage in society.

2. From line 6 to line 12, it should be understood that according to Edward Tenner:

(A) Technology is a brake to real progress.

(B) There is no progress without technology.

(C) The unintended consequences of information technology may have positive aspects.

(D) Unintended consequences may be avoided.

3. From line 6 to line 12, it should be understood that according to Evgeny Morazov:

(A) Intended consequences are all positive.

(B) Surveillance is part of the positive consequences.

(C) Not all intended consequences are positive.

(D) Authoritarian control is one of the noblest consequences.

4. From line 13 to line 21, it should be understood that technology:

(A) means no freedom.

(B) will never enslave us.

(C) is very helpful at work.

(D) has definitely increased our freedom.

5. From line 22 to line 31, it should be understood that:

(A) Leisure is spoiled by technology.

(B) Free time is more than ever tech-free.

(C) Social networks are becoming less and less attractive.

(D) Tech addiction is decreasing.

6. From line 22 to line 31, it should be understood that:

(A) There is no productivity without technology.

(B) Technology aims at making us happy.

(C) You cannot be happy if you are not fit.

(D) Technology has no impact on our body.`

7. From line 32 to line 41, it should be understood that:

(A) Technology makes our dreams come true.

(B) Technology helps us fall in love.

(C) Technology cannot be criticized.

(D) Technology creates a feeling of frustration.

8. From line 32 to line 41, it should be understood that:

(A) The characters shown on the web reflect reality.

(B) Virtual life is quite different from reality.

(C) You can easily identify with your fictional characters.

(D) You should believe what you see on the web.

9. From line 32 to line 41, it should be understood that:

(A) Being tech-addicted is pleasant.

(B) Nobody tries to fight against tech addiction.

(C) It is quite easy to get rid of tech gadgets.

(D) The internet can be solution to our tech addiction.

10. From line 42 to line 52, it should be understood that according to Theodor Adorno:

(A) Free time is fully relaxing.

(B) The border between free time and work is blurred.

(C) Free time enables you to cut off from work.

(D) It is easier to resume work after enjoying free time.

11. From line 42 to line 52, it should be understood that:

(A) The notion of citizenship is closely linked to the wellness industry.

(B) The leisure sector is losing customers.

(C) The wellness industry urges us to consume more and more.

(D) The wellness industry is close to bankrupt.

12. From line 42 to line 52, it should be understood that digital technology:

(A) triggers contradictory feelings.

(B) is no source of complaint.

(C) is more a source of hate than love.

(D) has nothing to do with tyranny.

II. LEXIQUE

Choisissez la réponse qui vous paraît la plus appropriée en fonction du contexte.

13. downright (line 2) means:

(A) fairly

(B) completely

(C) dangerously

(D) tiringly

14. moguls (line 5) means:

(A) pirates

(B) inhabitants

(C) kings

(D) movies

15. downplaying (line 10) means:

(A) ignoring

(B) minimising

(C) forgetting

(D) distorting

16. upshots (line 11) means:

(A) problems

(B) targets

(C) debates

(D) consequences

17. peevish (line 19) means:

(A) useless

(B) understandable

(C) old-fashioned

(D) vicious

18. harried (line 21) means:

(A) focused

(B) harrassed

(C) fascinated

(D) busy

19. suboptimal (line 30) means:

(A) creative

(B) obedient

(C) inferior

(D) addicted

20. breeds (line 33) means:

(A) targets

(B) ignores

(C) reflects

(D) engenders

21. woebegone (line 35) means:

(A) sad

(B) courteous

(C) smart

(D) happy

22. deflecting (line 41) means:

(A) turning away

(B) leading

(C) showing

(D) reducing

23. prying from (line 42) means:

(A) begging from

(B) gaining from

(C) break away from

(D) learning from

24. behemoth (line 46) means:

(A) competitor

(B) giant

(C) sector

(D) attraction

III. COMPETENCE GRAMMATICALE

Parmi les quatre phrases proposées, choisissez celle qui est grammaticalement correcte.

25.

(A) It is said this device to be dangerous.

(B) It is said that this device be dangerous.

(C) This device is said to be dangerous.

(D) This device is told to be dangerous.

26.

(A) There is lots more information to use.

(B) There are lot more informations to use.

(C) There is a lot more information to use.

(D) There are a lot more informations to use.

27.

(A) It's all the more easy as you just have to click.

(B) It's all the easier than you just have to click.

(C) It's all the easiest than you just have to click.

(D) It's all the easier as you just have to click.

28.

(A) They ought to have repaired it earlier.

(B) They ought have repaired it earlier.

(C) They ought to repair it earlier.

(D) They ought repaired it earlier.

29.

(A) A great many people are addicted to it.

(B) Many a great people are addicted to it.

(C) Great a many people are addicted to it.

(D) Great many people are addicted to it.

30.

(A) Should you need help, please let us know.

(B) If you should need help, please let us know.

(C) Should any help you need, please let us know.

(D) Any help you should need, please let us know.

31.

(A) Please check the button before you started.

(B) Please check the button before start.

(C) Please check the button before you've started.

(D) Please check the button before starting.

32.

(A) If I have money, I would buy it.

(B) If I had money, I would buy it.

(C) If I have had money, I would buy it.

(D) If I have money, I would have buy it.

Parmi les quatre solutions proposées, choisissez, pour chacun des énoncés lacunaires suivants celle qui vous paraît le compléter correctement.

33. ... on the net?

(A) Since how long are you surfing

(B) How long have you been surfing

(C) Since how long do you surf

(D) How long you surf

34. ... call me at once.

(A) When you will finish,

(B) When you have finished,

(C) When you will have finished,

(D) When you had finished,

35. … web surfers visit this site.

(A) Hundreds and hundreds

(B) Hundred and hundred

(C) Hundreds and hundreds of

(D) Hundred and hundred of

36. However …, don't believe it!

(A) true it may seem

(B) it may seem true

(C) true may it seem

(D) may it seem true

37. They ... their policy a decade ago.

(A) have reviewed

(B) have review

(C) had review

(D) reviewed

38. The company ... a lot since it was created.

(A) invests

(B) has invested

(C) has invest

(D) invested

39. You … understand everything.

(A) don't need

(B) needn't to

(C) don't need

(D) needn't

Corrigé Sujet e3a 2016 : Synthèse

Inconvenient truths about the gender gap, and a possible way out

Prejudices about men and women are mostly to blame for the gender gap in the workplace. What prejudices, and how to overcome them, is the focus of the set : Document 1, published in *The Guardian* in 2014 shows the UK walking backwards on the road to gender equality, while the US is slower than expected, if document 3, from *the Huffington Post* in 2015 is to be believed. This is due to a number of set ideas about men and women's roles, also described in document 2, from *The Telegraph* in 2015, and document 4 from the 2010 study *American Society: How It Actually Works.*

Documents 1 and 3 are clear that the goals set years ago in the US and the UK for more equal representation of women in key positions and in boards of directors haven't been met. The UK is even receding in world rankings for gender equality because it has failed to fix inequality in the workplace. One study shows only 17% of women are found in the 'chief' jobs in America, although women account for 45 % of the sample companies' workforce at entry level.

It all originates in preconceived ideas in both men and women. For instance, men supposedly have better leadership skills, according to a poll in document 3 ; however, this could be explained by an overwhelming majority of men's holding executive positions ; besides, men's competence is overestimated, while women's is underestimated. This results in women's not applying for higher positions, as they don't wish to be exposed to the extra pressure to perform. Nevertheless, still according to document 3, the notion that women tend to be unreliable because of motherhood is a misconception : more mothers stick to their jobs than childless women. The problem is representations about women and work : women are expected to be more burdened by their family life than men. Women also suffer from prejudices about their 'personality/competence ratio', which men don't have to face. A man working with women gets easy promotion, while the reverse isn't true.

The way this can be overcome is through efforts towards more equality in pay and benefits for men and women, according to document 4. Indeed, equal pay and equal parental leave would give men too more life choices. Document 2 also suggests developing the cultural habit to regard and value people as individuals, not as gender stereotypes. As per document 1, transparency about what is really going on in companies is also a good way to raise awareness and incite them to improve. (437 words title included, about 18 words/line)

Corrigé QCM e3a 2016

Rappel du barème :

Bonne réponse= +3

mauvaise réponse= -1

pas de réponse ou réponses multiples = 0

Pour calculer votre note finale de QCM sur 20 vous devez donc diviser votre total de points de COMPREHENSION par 3,6, celui de LEXIQUE par 7,2 et celui de COMPETENCE GRAMMATICALE par 9, puis faire la somme de ces trois résultats.

I. COMPREHENSION

1. From line 1 to line 5, it should be understood that technology:

(D) has caused great damage in society.

2. From line 6 to line 12, it should be understood that according to Edward Tenner:

(C) The unintended consequences of information technology may have positive aspects.

3. From line 6 to line 12, it should be understood that according to Evgeny Morazov:

(C) Not all intended consequences are positive.

4. From line 13 to line 21, it should be understood that technology:

(D) has definitely increased our freedom.

5. From line 22 to line 31, it should be understood that:

(A) Leisure is spoiled by technology.

6. From line 22 to line 31, it should be understood that:

(B) Technology aims at making us happy.

7. From line 32 to line 41, it should be understood that:

(D) Technology creates a feeling of frustration.

8. From line 32 to line 41, it should be understood that:

(B) Virtual life is quite different from reality.

9. From line 32 to line 41, it should be understood that:

(B) Nobody tries to fight against tech addiction.

10. From line 42 to line 52, it should be understood that according to Theodor Adorno:

(B) The border between free time and work is blurred.

11. From line 42 to line 52, it should be understood that:

(A) The notion of citizenship is closely linked to the wellness industry.

12. From line 42 to line 52, it should be understood that digital technology:

(A) triggers contradictory feelings.

.

II. LEXIQUE

13. downright (line 2) means:

(B) completely

14. moguls (line 5) means:

(C) kings

15. downplaying (line 10) means:

(B) minimising

16. upshots (line 11) means:

(D) consequences

17. peevish (line 19) means:

(D) vicious

18. harried (line 21) means:

(B) harrassed

19. suboptimal (line 30) means:

(C) inferior

20. breeds (line 33) means:

(D) engenders

21. woebegone (line 35) means:

(A) sad

22. deflecting (line 41) means:

(A) turning away

23. prying from (line 42) means:

(B) gaining from

24. behemoth (line 46) means:

(B) giant

III. COMPETENCE GRAMMATICALE

Parmi les quatre phrases proposées, choisissez celle qui est grammaticalement correcte.

25.

(C) This device is said to be dangerous.

26..

(C) There is a lot more information to use.

27.

(D) It's all the easier as you just have to click.

28.

(A) *They ought to have repaired it earlier.*

29.

(A) *A great many people are addicted to it.*

30.

(A) *Should you need help, please let us know.*

31.

(D*) Please check the button before starting.*

32.

(B) *If I had money, I would buy it.*

Parmi les quatre solutions proposées, choisissez, pour chacun des énoncés lacunaires suivants, celle qui vous paraît le compléter correctement.

33. … on the net?

(B) *How long have you been surfing*

34. ... call me at once.

(*B*) *When you have finished,*

35. … web surfers visit this site.

(C) *Hundreds and hundreds of*

36. However …, don't believe it!

(A*) true it may seem*

37. They ... their policy a decade ago.

(D) *reviewed*

38. The company ... a lot since it was created.

(*B) has invested*

39. You … understand everything.

(D) *needn't*

Sujet Mines Ponts 2016

Consignes

L'épreuve de langue vivante est constituée, d'un THÈME, et d'un EXERCICE D'EXPRESSION ECRITE qui n'est pas un exercice de contraction et qui consiste à répondre à deux questions.

- ! Le thème est noté sur 8.

- ! La première question est notée sur 4.

- ! La deuxième question est notée sur 8.

<u>La réponse à la première question devra comporter 80 mots plus ou moins 10%.</u>

Elle permet d'évaluer la compréhension du texte et la capacité des candidats à s'exprimer avec leurs propres mots.

<u>La réponse à la deuxième question devra comporter 180 mots plus ou moins 10%.</u>

Plus ouverte, elle permet d'apprécier les qualités d'expression, de jugement et d'argumentation. Dans les deux questions de l'exercice d'expression écrite, le candidat indiquera lui-même le nombre

de mots employés dans sa réponse. Le non respect des limites indiquées sera sanctionné. Les candidats sont priés de mentionner en tête de leur copie la langue dans laquelle ils ont composé.

Sujet Mines Ponts 2016

Jeff Bezos, Rocket Man

Fifty-eight years after Sputnik, a new space race is unfolding. This time, instead of nuclear-armed superpowers, the protagonists are trash-talking billionaires. But the outcome may one day prove as electrifying as the moon landings.

This week, Blue Origin LLC, the secretive space company backed by Jeff Bezos of Amazon.com, launched an unmanned vehicle called the New Shepherd to the edge of outer space. A short time later, the rocket that propelled it parachuted down in the West Texas desert – four feet from where it took off, and all in one piece. It was, Bezos declared, "a game changer." That's only a slight exaggeration.

Since the dawn of the Space Age, rockets have been treated as a regrettably disposable byproduct of getting a payload into orbit. The cost of this waste has been an impediment to expanding travel and business opportunities in space. A reliably reusable rocket could change that calculus drastically. Elon Musk – proprietor of SpaceX, one of Blue Origin's competitors – thinks it could reduce expenses by a factor of 100.

As clashes of billionaires go, this is a tame and encouraging one. And it comes at a propitious time. Space is suddenly brimming with commercial possibilities, spurred by a new generation of small and cheap satellites. A company called Planet Labs is connecting a network of satellites for use in agriculture and disaster relief. PlanetiQ wants to improve climate monitoring and weather forecasting. Other companies hope to validate insurance claims, analyze retail trends and offer worldwide Internet access from space.

Reusable rockets could make such endeavors far cheaper. They may even make more esoteric pursuits – from asteroid mining to colonizing the cosmos – more realistic. And their best uses probably haven't occurred to anyone yet.

Bezos and Musk are at the vanguard of this revolution. They're exporting Silicon Valley's competitive ethos to outer space, spurring creative new industries and giving government space agencies a much-needed jolt. They'll surely have setbacks along the way. But that's how progress works. (337 words)

adapted from *Bloomberg*, November 25, 2015

Question 1 : According to the article, how are current developments in the space industry "a game changer" ? Answer the question in your own words. (80 words +/- 10 percent)

Question 2 : In your opinion, why does mankind continue to be fascinated by space ? Illustrate your answer with relevant examples. (180 words +/- 10 percent)

Thème

Un dimanche après la messe, j'avais douze ans, avec mon père, j'ai monté le grand escalier de la mairie. On a cherché la porte de la bibliothèque municipale. Jamais nous n'y étions allés. Je m'en faisais une fête. On n'entendait aucun bruit derrière la porte. Mon père l'a poussée, toutefois. C'était silencieux, le parquet craquait. Deux hommes nous regardaient venir depuis un comptoir trèshaut barrant l'accès aux rayons. Mon père m'a laissé demander : « On voudrait emprunter des livres. » L'un des hommes aussitôt: « Qu'est-ce que vous voulez comme livres ? »

A la maison, on n'avait pas pensé qu'il fallait savoir d'avance ce qu'on voulait, être capable de citer des titres aussi facilement que des marques de biscuits.

On a choisi à notre place. Nous ne sommes pas retournés à la bibliothèque. C'est ma mère qui a dû rendre les livres, peut-être, avec du retard. (150 words)

Annie Ernaux, La place (1983)

Corrigé Sujet Mines-Ponts 2016 : expression écrite

Question 1 : According to the article, how are current developments in the space industry "a game changer" ? Answer the question in your own words. (80 words +/- 10 percent, 4 points)

What has changed since the Moon landing age is that private players, such as billionaires Bezos and Musk, are now in the race to space, and they have brought their Silicon Valley zest for profitability into the game. This means that savings can be made which will encourage an increasing number of companies to play the space card thanks to cheap satellites and launcher rockets, turning space into a real new Frontier. Opportunities to use space for cheap will create new, unforeseen uses for space. (85 words)

Question 2 : In your opinion, why does mankind continue to be fascinated by space ? Illustrate your answer with relevant examples. (180 words +/- 10 percent, 8 points)

Elon Musk has dreams about colonizing Mars, and he is probably traducing a form of anxiety many people have about the limitations of our small planet, whereas space is infinite. For Americans in particular, the Frontier epic is still vivid, and it is frustrating that there should no longer be new territories to be conquered on Earth. The fascination of space is its infinity. As the phrase goes, « the sky is the limit ». We look to space as the place of absolute opportunity, maybe as a metaphor of the human potential itself which we cannot really fulfill on this crowded ,over-exploited planet. The idea that somewhere, maybe, there is another, pristine planet Earth to be found and explored is very appealing.

Perhaps the very good science fiction we have enjoyed in novels and movies has something to do with the fascination too. The wonderful works of Isaac Asimov with his *Foundation* trilogy and robot stories, Ray Bradbury with his *Martian Chronicles*, and Frank Herbert with *Dune*, as well as the *Star Wars* Cycle have made space colonization very attractive to the human imagination. Space is limitless, like our imagination, that is why we love it. (198 words)

Corrigé Sujet Mines-Ponts 2016 : thème (8 points)

One Sunday after Mass, when I was 12, I climbed (1) the main Town Hall stairway with my father. We looked for the door of the public (2) library. We had never been there before. I was really looking forward to it. There was no noise from behind the door. Nevertheless, my father pushed it. It was silent in there, the wooden floor creaked. Two men watched us as we came, from a very high counter barring the way to the bookshelves. My father let me put our request : 'We would like to borrow books.' In a flash, one of the men said (3): 'What books d'you want ?'

Back home, we hadn' t thought onc had to know in advance what one wanted and be able to name (4) titles the way one would a brand of biscuits. They chose for us. We didn't go back to the library. I guess it was my mother who took the books back, late.

(1) *variante* : I went up

(2) *var* : municipal library

(3) *var:* tit for tat, one of the men said

(4) *var* : to quote titles

II. SUJETS D'ENTRAINEMENT

SUJET X-ENS N°1

ÉPREUVE ÉCRITE DE LANGUE VIVANTE

ANGLAIS

Durée totale de l'épreuve écrite de langue vivante (A+B) : 4 heures

Documents autorisés : aucun

PREMIÈRE PARTIE (A) : SYNTHÈSE DE DOCUMENTS

Contenu du dossier : trois articles et un document iconographique. Les documents sont numérotés 1, 2, 3 et 4.

Sans paraphraser les documents proposés dans le dossier, le candidat réalisera une synthèse decelui-ci, en mettant clairement en valeur ses principaux enseignements et enjeux dans le contexte de l'aire géographique de la langue choisie, et en prenant soin de n'ajouter aucun commentaire personnel à sa composition.

La synthèse proposée devra comprendre entre 600 et 675 mots et sera rédigée intégralement dans la langue choisie. Elle sera en outre obligatoirement précédée d'un titre proposé par le candidat.

SECONDE PARTIE (B) : TEXTE D'OPINION

En réagissant aux arguments exprimés dans cet éditorial (document numéroté 5), le candidat rédigera lui-même dans la langue choisie un texte d'opinion d'une longueur de 500 à 600 mots.

A – Document 1

Pokémon Go drives a few points home about Augmented Reality

Alexander M. Jacob, *Synthesis*

10 October 2016

I've had a good time lately reading how the Pokémon Go mania had invited itself in the battle over National Health Service cuts in the UK. Gamers have been getting out of the couch with obvious benefits in the shape of weight loss and muscle building ; which immediately led some to speculate that this could ultimately save the NHS money (read : justify more cuts, « horror, horror », quoth the Guardian). Now seriously. The most relevant of all conversations started by Pokemon Go is about space, not calorie or NHS cuts.

If party poopers are to be believed, the Pokémon scavenger hunt entails invasion of private or « sacred » grounds by hordes of insensitive rucksack carriers. The game superimposes a digital layer to your surroundings, creating a new space in which the laws of the « real » urban world somehow cease to apply.

It's not exactly as if the pokémon trainer stepped into a lawless dimension. It's more as if modern urban conventions, privacy and property laws had been somehow displaced by a more rural law, or maybe a throwback to the age-old agreements that included « right of game» for hunters. If the prey runs into private property, the real hunter has a right to trespass in pursuit. Judging by the number of trespassing and breach of privacy incidents since July 7, the massification of Augmented Reality is set to change the rules.

Some Augmented Reality purists are arguing that Pokémon Go is not real AR, more like à location-based game or « mixed reality » but actually this isn't the point. The point is that Pokémon Go has helped Augmented Reality go mainstream overnight in a massive sort of way, and thereby raised the question of the multiplication, or superimposition, of spaces which is poised to become a fact of our lives.

Augmented Reality is bound to create a whole new Frontier of legal tangles that is enough to make any jurist's mouth water. Do laws that apply to tangible space apply to Augmented space ? Who owns Augmented spaces ? And so on. Those who think it should be easy to demarcate real-world no-go areas are wrong. The Pokémon Go boom stands to attract exploiters, starting with retailer events and promotional tie-ins, and   the game is only the tip of the Augmented

Reality iceberg. The push to stretch our common space will be irresistible and conflicts are inevitable.

I want to take my analogy with the American Frontier further. It strikes me that Pokémon Go was designed in Silicon Valley, California, historically the ultimate pioneering land. California was also, not coincidentally, the tangible limit to the coast-to-coast drive westward : when the Pacific Ocean was reached, the conquest of the West was by and large over.

America took the news of the official end of the Frontier in 1890 with shock and awe. If the nation's « manifest destiny » was no longer to be on the move, conquering virgin territory, what next ? The answer was « new Frontiers » of a different nature. President Kennedy forcefully articulated this in his 1960 acceptance speech at the Democratic Convention: the new Frontier was going to be technology and outer space. The space odyssey has since lost momentum and lustre mostly owing to astronomical costs. But technology is currently creating the new Frontiers under our eyes. Those California geeks, they just won't give up on The Dream.

Indeed, Augmented Reality has the potential to create new Frontiers at comparatively low cost. At a time when capitalism is running into the physical limitations of our planet in terms of resources and even space, it makes it possible to create whole virgin « territories » for the smart and resourceful, just like in the good old days. Go Augmented, young man, strike gold in your own nondescript neighbourhood by developing the app that brings in revenue from a wild layer of space you own and superimpose on space you do not own. That is the trick. Infinity is the limit.

Infinite versions of a finite space... This is where augmented Reality invites itself in another big conversation of our time, ie 'the one v. the many'. Some commentators have pointed out that no matter how fleeting comradeship may arise between hunters, Pokémon Go alienates people from each other even further, and there is a risk that the multiplication of AR apps will compound this.

What with the customization of Augmented Reality that might enable everyone to overlay the outside world with their own preferences. Our societies are already atomized and solipsistic enough, and now will we end up with a socially deserted real world while everyone around is moving inside their Augmented own ? Besides, Pokémon Go is just a harmless game with cute characters, but there is no guarantee that all AR apps will be so. Some of them could encourage downright antisocial feelings or even behaviour, or worse.

Now, AR-based game and fun apps will no doubt multiply, but as far as « serious » or useful applications are concerned, I see the future as association rather than dissociation. The vanishing of the Frontier in the US coincided with the rise of industrial and capitalistic concentration, and after the pioneering times, something like this will happen to Augmented Reality as it did to operating systems and social networks. Concentration, not dispersion.

Some kind of platform, or maybe two or three of them, are bound to emerge that will conveniently cull and centralize most of the relevant Augmentation of any given spot. Including an Augmented wiki that one switches on when one arrives. Moreover AR has a rich potential for sharing and collaborative undertakings, from real-time warnings to surgery, emergency, repair and control operations. Most of us will probably stick to that, so does it matter if some creeps still walk around with phones that make every passer-by look like a zombie or a target? I don't think so. They'll grow out of it, as I suspect people will grow tired of Pokémon Go pretty soon.

The advent of AR may not solve our real-life problems of space and resources on this cramped little planet, nor our alienation from each other, but it certainly won't make matters worse. So all in all Pokémon Go is more good news than bad. (1058)

A – Document 2

Pokémon Go is just the start

Silicon Valley is taking over our reality

Srecko Horvat, *The Guardian*

Monday 25 July 2016

(...) Never before has digital reality become so integrated into our physical world.

It has even become part of the US presidential elections, with Hillary Clinton chiming in that she doesn't "know who created Pokémon Go, but I'd try to figure out how to get them to have Pokémon go to the polls". In truth Clinton knows very well who created Pokémon Go. It was her friends in Silicon Valley.

How to explain the success of Pokémon Go? One way is to follow the money, and it might be easier to explain. Augmented reality (AR) is not something new; it has been used for years in the military and for navigation systems. What makes Pokémon Go novel is that AR has gone mainstream for the first time. And it has to be understood as a historical break, which will profoundly change the way we perceive and experience reality. It will change reality itself.(...)

Pokémon Go wouldn't be possible without Google

Pokémon Go was created by Niantic, whose director John Hanke was one of the founders of Keyhole – a pioneering software development company specialised in geospatial data visualisation that paved the way for Google Maps and Google Earth. Keyhole was acquired by Google in 2004, as was Niantic. Pokémon Go wouldn't be possible without Google. After Google Glass received massive criticism and legislative action due to privacy and safety concerns, it can even be seen as a first successful commercial step in the direction of enabling Google's AR dream.

And this is why the faux-naivety of what Hillary Clinton says about this is important. She must know that it is the former CEO of Google, Eric Schmidt, who is running the digital component of her own campaign, using a startup known as The Groundwork. And she must know that Schmidt recently became head of the Pentagon's innovation board and that between January 2009 and October 2015, Google's top executives and representatives gathered at the White House on 427 separate occasions. Obviously there is a symbiotic relationship between the US state department and Silicon Valley. But why should this worry us?

We don't have to speculate about what Silicon Valley's ideology is, it is enough to read Peter Thiel's *Zero to One: Notes on Startups, or How to Build the Future*. Thiel, part of the so-called "Paypal mafia" and owner of Palantir, explicitly says that "competition is a relic of history" and that monopoly capitalism is not a pathology or an exception, but the condition of every successful business. Google is one of the best examples: almost all of Google's "innovations" are a product of acquisition (from Google Maps to Youtube).

Another successful example, mentioned by Thiel himself, is Tesla Motors: "Tesla's technology is so good that other car companies rely on it: Daimler uses Tesla's battery packs; Mercedes Benz uses a Tesla powertrain; Toyota uses a Tesla motor. General Motors has even created a taskforce to track Tesla's next moves. But Tesla's greatest technological achievement isn't one single component, but rather its ability to integrate many components into one superior product."

This is the best description of monopoly capitalism. The success of Silicon Valley is not a result of genius, but purchase – Google, Facebook, Apple or Palantir succeeded in creating such powerful and pervasive monopolies precisely because of such acquisitions.

Pokémon Go marks a further step, because the penetration of Silicon Valley into the most intimate aspects of our lives through social networks and new technology has reached a level in which our physical reality becomes integrated into the digital reality. Soon it will be impossible to distinguish the physical from the digital, realising the idea behind Google Glass.

Pokémon Go should be viewed as an important breakthrough that can't be defined properly without taking into consideration the total colonisation undertaken by Silicon Valley through the "internet of things" (absolute integration of our vehicles, homes, tools into the network), "smart cities" (acquisition of our cities' infrastructure by Silicon Valley), social networks (Facebook, Twitter, Instagram), Google, transport innovations (drones, Tesla Motors, etc), "big data", total surveillance, AI, VR, and last but not least, immortality (Silicon Valley's dream that we will upload our brains and live forever).

All these fields of massive investment and radical innovation transform our reality in such a profound way that every aspect of our lives will soon be integrated into a big global digital "network" which is already, for the first time in human history, enabling the creation of a constantly interconnected global brain.

The problem is not technology or innovation, the problem is monopoly capitalism: the fact that all this power is concentrated in a few companies from Silicon Valley, who openly want to create a brave new world in which technology only serves profit. While we're all busy playing Pokémon, the companies are following the game's advice – "Gotta catch 'em all". Only, its us being captured in an inescapable web of technological consumerism. (820 words, edited)

A – Document 3

Pokémon Go:

Who owns the virtual space around your home?

Alex Hern, *The Guardian*

Wednesday 13 July 2016

(...)In the Sydney suburb of Rhodes, a chance confluence of Pokéstops has led to "hundreds" of players milling around a small outdoor area. "The place is in complete chaos with crowds of well over 1,000 per night. There is a massive level of noise after midnight, uncontrollable traffic, excessive rubbish, smokers, drunk people, people who are 'camping' in the site, and even people peddling mobile phone chargers," a resident told Buzzfeed.

Boon Sheridan, a Massachusetts man who lives in a converted church, has found his house has been designated a Pokémon Gym, the most important category of locations in the game. For days, people have been loitering outside his house, leaving him concerned it "could easily make this place look like a dealer's house".

Some of these problems can be pegged to the unexpected, astronomical success of Pokémon Go. Back in June, I spoke to John Hanke, the chief executive and cofounder of the game's developers, Niantic Labs.(..) When asked about future plans, Hanke instead discussed licensing the core technology behind Pokémon Go to other brands looking to make their own AR games. That's likely to still be on the cards, but for now, the company has their hands full dealing with the monster they've unleashed.

Naivety can't be the only excuse, though. Niantic Labs has been doing this for a long time. Ingress, a science fiction-tinged game developed back when the company was still a subsidiary of Google, has been running for six and half years. In July 2015, the company faced an almost identical controversy, after the German magazine Zeit reported that concentration and death camps including Dachau, Buchenwald and Auschwitz-Birkenau were all set up as in-game "portals". Some were deleted the day after Zeit contacted Google; others remained, including a portal specifically located at the notorious "Arbeit Macht Frei" gates in Auschwitz.

Pokémon Go and Ingress share a database, built over half a decade from a mixture of public information sources and volunteer contributions. In a technical sense, it's little different from

Wikipedia: a database of geotagged entries on points of interest dotted around the world.(...)

Wikipedia, of course, can be edited by anyone. Niantic's database cannot. For the first few days, the company would only accept reports about physical locations "that present immediate physical danger (for example, they are in the middle of a road or on railroad tracks)". Now, the company has widened it out, and users can report an issue for a number of reasons, including, notably, to highlight a Pokéstop "on private property".

The language is telling, and may give more ground – real or virtual – than Niantic intended. A Pokéstop cannot be "on private property". A Pokéstop does not exist: it is a latitude and longitude stored on Niantic's servers, interpreted by the Pokémon Go client which then represents it as a circle hovering over a stylised Google Map of the area surrounding the player.

In the short term, it clearly makes sense for Niantic to offer this control to landowners. It doesn't result in great press for your megaviral casual game if players are arrested for trespassing due to the instructions the game gives them.

Niantic can also comfort itself with the fact that a number of properties are quite happy with their inclusion in the game. Churches have been reported making the most of the sudden influx of young secular players; signs have popped up outside shops reading "No purchase, no Pokémon" and "come for the Pokémon, stay for the selection of retro clothes at affordable prices"; and bars and pubs have found that even if they aren't an official Pokéstop, dropping a lure on-site results in a short-lived flood of Pokémon.(...)

But even though the interests of Niantic and landowners happen to coincide for now, there's no guarantee that state of affairs is universal. And if – or rather, when – the edge-case arrives, it's not entirely clear what the right response is. Who does own the virtual space around you? I can't put a billboard on your house without asking you; but is it so obvious that I should be allowed to put a virtual billboard "on" your house without giving you any say in the matter?(...)

Perhaps the best thing to do is to look backwards, not forward, for solutions. In the early days of the 20th century, another technological revolution raised questions of control, trespass and oversight: the aeroplane.

Who owns the air above the land? For millennia, the answer had been both obvious and irrelevant.(...)

The specifics of that answer vary around the world, but the generalities are the same: above a certain height, the airspace is owned by the state. Landowners can't charge pilots for the privilege of flying over their land, nor can they block it off entirely.

But there's a quid pro quo. States enforce a responsibility to the people on the ground, ensuring that unsafe vehicles don't fly overhead, limiting the noise emitted by low-flying planes, particularly overnight, and ideally ensuring that access to the skies isn't held hostage for private profit.

In the virtual world, nations are already approaching the same compromise. Data protection laws, particularly in Europe, allow for the freedom to innovate while still offering individuals the choice to object. It's not a stretch that soon you'll be able to denote your home a sort of digital no-fly zone, requesting its exemption from databases like Niantic's without requiring you to individually negotiate a deal with every single AR company.

Technology has typically outpaced legislation, and even with tens of millions of downloads it doesn't look like Pokémon Go will be the tipping point that causes that trend to change. But the questions raised over the past few days aren't going away, and while a wild west may work for some, it's ultimately unsustainable.(966 words, edited)

Document 4

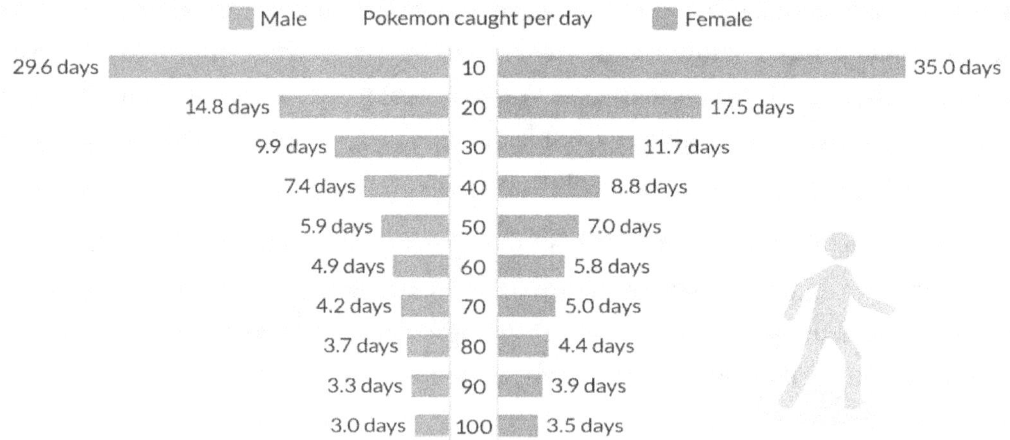

US MINUTES PER ACTIVE POKÉMON GO USER ONE WEEK PRIOR & ONE WEEK AFTER THE LAUNCH - COMPARED WITH OTHER POPULAR APPS IN 2016

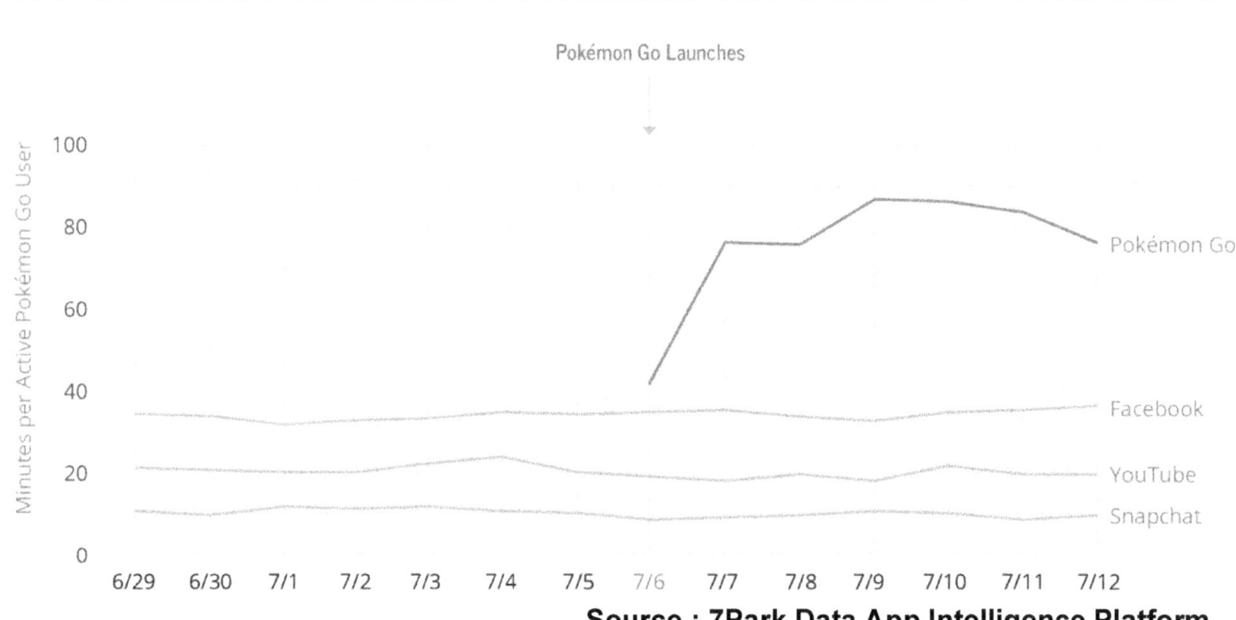

Source : 7Park Data App Intelligence Platform

Sujet B – Document 5

Why Pokémon Go is a game-changer for us all

Hari Kunzru, *The Guardian*

Monday 1 August 2016

(...)The idea of augmented reality (AR) has been around for years, and the smartphone is finally allowing developers to make apps that overlay your local street, park and bus stop with extra visuals or information that can enhance or transform them.

(...)A little searching offers all sorts of other current AR possibilities. Some are useful – point your phone at a foreign road sign or a menu and get an instant translation. Others sound crass and depressing. Do I want to "convert anything in the real world into an interactive 'wow' experience"? Not really, because the real world is already interactive and more full of wonders than anyone who uses the word "wow" as an adjective is likely to understand.

So far, many of the available applications are aimed squarely at advertisers (the "wow experience" app seems to be a tool for making AR ads), and the prospect of navigating a reality that has commercials embedded into its very fabric is not enticing. But consolations occur. The walking tour of your city where you see how it looked 100 years ago. The ramble in the woods where taxonomical information about the trees hovers in the branches …

And yet there's a deeply ingrained moral reflex that suggests to us that the world ought to be enough. We have cultural traditions intended to inoculate us against the flight into artificial paradises (just say no, kids!), or cutting ourselves off from the social reality of our fellows. Science fiction offers various dystopian visions of isolation in which the everyday turns out to be an illusion, and we are "really" tethered in stalls in some nightmarish factory farm or distracting ourselves as we scrape out a living in a burning, post-apocalyptic wasteland. These stories warn that if the real becomes mutable or untrustworthy, our experience of ourselves (not to mention each other) may become insubstantial, that what makes life meaningful is a certain intractability, a resistance to our desires.

(...)Although while I may wish to augment my reality with nerdy explanatory wall texts and elevating historical overlays, there's no guarantee that my neighbour may not prefer to move through a world overlaid with grotesque violence or extreme pornography, or just exist in some 24/7 Snapchat-esque fever dream in which everyone looks like cartoon dogs. What happens when we're in the same physical space, but in all other respects, we have ceased to share much of anything at all? And what does it mean if someone elects to screen out certain aspects of their environment? Poverty, for example, or disabled people, or women's uncovered faces?

This is where the ethics of reality augmentation will begin to intersect with an idea much discussed in political circles, the "filter bubble", a phrase coined by activist Eli Pariser for our tendency to create an echo chamber around ourselves, to reinforce ideas and perceptions that we appreciate, and mute those we find disturbing or contrary to our prejudices.

Last year a paper was published by computer scientists at the University of Southern California describing the mathematical basis for what they call "the majority illusion". Because of the structure of our social networks, behaviour or attitudes that are perhaps not common at all globally may appear to us to be "what everybody thinks" or "what everybody's doing". Individual choices are strongly influenced by the behaviour of friends and peers, whether that's getting a new phone, joining a social movement, or chewing weird berries. Contagion is rife, creating menswear fashions or suicide clusters.

Our "self-evident" perceptions of the world – the self-evidence that leads us to believe skinny jeans are cool or sleeping pills are the only solution – may be highly skewed, and have little in common with the perceptions of those enmeshed in networks far away.

(…) In the current American election campaign, and indeed in Britain, filter bubbles of extreme constriction and resilience are in evidence on left and right. Social media has allowed people to create hashtag bunkers for themselves. The faux universality of these structures seems to have the curious psychological effect of reducing tolerance of dissenting views. Imagine the augmented version of this, a politics in which all participants inhabit their own highly tailored realities, and are in the process of forgetting that those realities are partially constructed, so "natural" and "intuitive" do they feel. It is unlikely to be an agora of democratic civility. In fact the agora, the shared space of the polis, will be precisely what has vanished.

Like previous technological waves, AR will probably be too useful to resist, even for people who have an instinctive horror of mediation. Though it won't plunge the people of the world into a solipsistic abyss, it is a development like that of the "internet of things" –

something which may appear superficially modish and insubstantial, a froth of gadgets and jargon – but whose possibilities to transform the social world are at least as profound as the internet wave of the last quarter century.

There are what technocrats like to term "challenges" ahead, not least for human freedom and dignity.(...) (845 words, edited)

SUJET X-ENS N°2

A – Document 1

Here comes the sun: US solar power market hits all-time high

Matt Weiser, The Guardian

Tuesday 28 June 2016

(…) Remarkably, the US solar energy industry is now entering what may be its most prosperous decade ever, thanks to a new wave of federal and state policies and positive economics in the industry, both at home and abroad.

"I think it will actually be bigger than people are projecting," says Jigar Shah, president and co-founder of Generate Capital, a clean energy investment firm based in San Francisco. "The solar industry is booming right now."

The US solar industry expects to install 14.5 gigawatts of solar power in 2016, a 94% increase over the record 7.5 gigawatts last year, according to a new market report by GTM Research and the Solar Energy Industries Association. Revenues from solar installations also increased 21% from 2014 to more than $22bn in 2015.

For the first time, more solar systems came online than natural gas power plants – the top source of electricity in the US – in 2015, as measured in megawatts, said Justin Baca, vice president of markets and research at the Solar Energy Industries Association. This year, new solar is expected to surpass installations of all other sources, said the US Energy Information Administration.

The rise of solar energy use, especially by homes and businesses with panels on their roofs, is gradually transforming the electricity industry. For more than a century, power plant owners and utilities have controlled the energy delivery service, and some of them enjoy a monopoly.

"We were just a tiny little speck 10 years ago, and now we are really up there with the major established generating technologies," said Baca. "It's amazing."

Sunny path

What's behind all this? A federal tax credit has played a key role: it enables home and business owners to take off 30% of the price of their solar energy systems from their income taxes. Congress renewed the tax credit last December.

Another factor is cost. It is simply a lot cheaper to install solar these days, largely because cost of components have declined considerably. The wholesale price of a solar panel today is about $0.65 per watt, compared with $0.74 per watt a year ago and $4 per watt in 2008.

(…) Can you power a business on

Then China, where labor costs were lower, rose to become a mighty manufacturing force. Chinese manufacturers built massive factories to make solar panels, drove down the prices for solar panels and forced more than a hundred of its competitors in Europe, US and even within China to go bankrupt.

The fallout hurt so many businesses that the US government imposed tariffs on Chinese-made solar panels (...).

The tariffs and increasing domestic demand have boosted manufacturing jobs in the US, which is now one of the top five nations for solar panel producers behind China, Singapore, Taiwan and Malaysia.

"Now the market's so large you can actually sustain the large manufacturing plants and support the product locally," said Shah.

One example is SolarCity, which is building a giant new solar panel factory in Buffalo, New York. The facility, expected to be in operation later this year, plans to employ 3,500 people. It will produce panels primarily for SolarCity's own projects around the world.

(…) Dark clouds ahead?

Although the solar market is booming overall, its reliance on government incentives makes it vulnerable to the whims of policymakers. In Nevada, once considered a role model for solar development and a national leader for solar jobs per capita, the state Public Utilities Commission approved a major rollback of solar subsidies and policies last December.

The commission voted in response to a complaint by the state's largest utility, NVEnergy, which contended that the subsidy – and the billing process required for the program – threatened its profitability.

That change prompted SolarCity, one of America's largest solar companies, to stop selling and installing new systems in Nevada and take some 550 jobs with it. Another company, Sunrun, did the same. As a result, the industry association expects Nevada to drop from the fifth-largest state for residential solar installations in 2015 to 31st by the end of this year.

Robert Boehm, director of the Center for EnergyResearch at the University of Nevada-Las Vegas, said the changes could mean trouble ahead for the industry as a whole.

(…) Energy storage presents another obstacle. Solar remains a small contributor to the nation's energy supply, accounting for less than 1% percent of total electricity production. As it grows and replaces traditional sources of energy, which can produce electricity any time, the need to make solar energy available even when the sun isn't shining will only grow.

Batteries are emerging to be the solution, but the technology and the manufacturing scale aren't improving quick enough to make it financially feasible for the masses. One company,Tesla Motors, is attempting to address that problem by building a massive factory in Nevada to build lithium-ion batteries that will go into energy storage packs designed by Tesla for homes and businesses.

"The amount of capital and investment going into solar is at an all-time high," Shah said. "I think the economics are clearly very good and we haven't really even tapped but a very small percentage of our opportunities." (865 words, edited)

A- Document 2

In Tesla and SolarCity Deal, a Glimpse of Musk's Clean-Energy Aspirations

By LESLIE PICKER and BILL VLASIC, *New York Times*

Aug 1, 2016

In the face of questions about debt, widening losses, governance and strategic logic, Tesla Motors and SolarCity announced a $2.6 billion stock merger on Monday.

Now, it is up to Elon Musk to persuade the shareholders of the two companies — he founded both — that the deal makes sense. The transaction requires the approval this year of a majority of shareholders from bothTesla and SolarCity, excluding Mr. Musk and other insiders

Completion of the deal may come down to whether enough investors have the patience to accept the near-term headaches while waiting for Mr. Musk's long-term vision.

His idea is that Tesla's batteries could store the power that SolarCity's panels have harnessed, a bet on the increasing use of solar energy. Most analysts, though, say this vision could take years, maybe even decades, to play out on a large scale — often longer than many investors tend to wait.

"I don't know why people would be voting in favor of it," said Efraim Levy, chief automotive analyst at Standard & Poor's Global Market Intelligence. "The valuation is excessive given the current prospects and the time horizon we're looking at."

But Mr. Musk, who also founded a third company with the hope of sending humans to Mars one day, is known for his visionary zeal. By doing this deal, he sees Tesla eventually moving beyond autos to become more of a clean-energy company that also happens to sell cars.

"This is really all part of solving the sustainable-
energy problem," Mr. Musk said in a conference
call with analysts on Monday. "That's why we're all doing this — is to try to accelerate the advent of a sustainable-energy world."

The prospects of a deal surfaced on June 20, when Tesla submitted a proposal to Lyndon Rive, the chief executive of SolarCity — and Mr. Musk's cousin — to acquire the company.

(…) Tesla, which will report its second-quarter earnings on Wednesday, is going through a major transition as a car company. It is expanding its assembly plant in California, in hopes of beginning to fill the more than 300,000 preorders for its coming Model 3 sedan by next year. To speed the process, Mr. Musk has overhauled his manufacturing team, bringing in new executives from rival automakers such as Audi.

(…) Monday's deal includes a so-called go-shop period, which enables SolarCity to continue soliciting proposals from other parties until Sept. 14.

The two companies plan to cut about $150 million in costs through the transaction in the first full year after the deal closes. They expect customers to benefit through lower hardware and installation costs, and they plan to use Tesla's 190 stores to expand SolarCity's reach.

Through Tesla's stores, SolarCity would get easier, cheaper access to millions of customers; SolarCity has struggled to reduce its customer acquisition costs. In addition, it could benefit from the carmaker's expertise in manufacturing, just as SolarCity prepares to produce its own solar panels at a heavily subsidized factory in Buffalo.

Mr. Rive, of SolarCity, said in the conference call that he expected almost all solar systems to include battery storage within three to five years, and that the combined company would be able to prosper by providing those systems, along with energy services for the grid. Adding rooftop solar to the overall energy mix, Mr. Musk said, would allow utility companies to avoid building new substations and transmission lines as the rising use of electric vehicles and heating systems increases demand for power.

The merger, he said, would help Tesla take better advantage of all the customers it attracts to its stores by offering them more products. Making the solar systems appealing, he said, was important.

Although some investors have expressed support for the deal, many analysts and investors have continued to question whether it makes sense for the carmaker to take on SolarCity, which has piled on debt as it seeks to continue its aggressive expansion. Last month, SolarCity said it had raised $345 million in tax-equity financing and added $110 million to a loan agreement, bringing its total to $760 million.

And on Monday, SolarCity reduced projections for residential system installations for 2016 by nearly 10 percent because the pace of installations had been slower than expected in the first half of the year.

Many analysts are still optimistic that, despite the risks, the deal will ultimately get done.

"Everything about Elon is for the long term," said David Whiston, an analyst with Morningstar. "I suspect the big, institutional shareholders understand that and they're all in on Elon, and I expect the large shareholders will vote yes for the deal."(771 words, edited)

A – Document 3

Preparing for large-scale solar deployment

Measures to ensure a reliable future power system

NANCY W. STAUFFER, *MITEI* (Massachusetts Institute of Technology Energy Initiative)

December 14, 2015

Most experts agree that solar power must be a critical component of any long-term plan to address climate change. By 2050, a major fraction of the world's power should come from solar sources. However, analyses performed as part of the MIT Future of Solar Energy study found that getting there won't be straightforward. "One of the big messages of the solar study is that the power system has to get ready for very high levels of solar PV generation," says Ignacio Pérez-Arriaga, a visiting professor at the MIT Sloan School of Management from IIT-Comillas University in Madrid, Spain.

Without the ability to store energy, all solar (and wind) power devices are intermittent sources of electricity. When the sun is shining, electricity produced by PVs flows into the power system, and other power plants can be turned down or off because their generation isn't needed. When the sunshine goes away, those other plants must come back online to meet demand. That scenario poses two problems. First, PVs send electricity into a system that was designed to deliver it, not receive it. And second, their behavior requires other power plants to operate in ways that may be difficult or even impossible.

The result is that solar PVs can have profound, sometimes unexpected impacts on operations, future investments, costs, and prices on both distribution systems—the local networks that deliver electricity to consumers—and bulk power systems—the large interconnected systems made up of generation and transmission facilities. And those impacts grow as the solar presence increases.

Supporting local distribution

To examine impacts on distribution networks, the researchers used the Reference Network Model (RNM), which was developed at IIT-Comillas and simulates the design and operation of distribution networks that transfer electricity from high-voltage transmission systems to all final consumers.

(...)In some situations, the addition of dispersed PV systems reduces the distance electricity must travel along power lines, so less is lost in transit and costs go down. But as the PV energy share grows, that benefit is eclipsed by the need to invest in reinforcing or modifying the existing network to handle two-way power flows. Changes could include installing larger transformers, thicker wires, and new voltage regulators or even reconfiguring the network, but the net result is added cost to protect both equipment and quality of service.

(...)The impact is also greater in less sunny regions. Indeed, in areas with low insolation, distribution costs may nearly double when the PV contribution exceeds one-third of annual load. The reason: When insolation is low, many more solar generating devices must be installed to meet a given level of demand, and the network needs to be ready to handle all the electricity flowing from those devices on the occasional sunny day.

One way to reduce the burden on distribution networks is to add local energy storage capability. Depending on the scenario and the storage capacity, at 30% PV penetration, storage can reduce added costs by a third in Europe and cut them in half in the United States. "That doesn't mean that deployment of storage is economically viable now," says Pérez-Arriaga. "Current storage technology is expensive, but one of the services with economic value that it can provide is to bring down the cost of deploying solar PV."

(…) Impacts on bulk power systems

In other work, the researchers focused on the impact of PV penetration on larger-scale electric systems. Using the Low Emissions Electricity Market Analysis model—another tool developed at IIT-Comillas—they examined how operations on bulk power systems, the future generation mix, and prices on wholesale electricity markets might evolve as the PV energy share grows.

(...)A typical bulk power system includes a variety of power plants with differing costs and characteristics. Conventional coal and nuclear plants are inexpensive to run (though expensive to build), but they don't switch on and off easily or turn up and down quickly. Plants fired by natural gas are more expensive to run (and less expensive to build), but they're also more flexible. In general, demand is met by dispatching the least expensive plants first and then turning to more expensive and flexible plants as needed.

(…) when the PV energy share reaches 58%, the solar generation pushes down net demand dramatically, such that when the sun goes down, other generators must go from low to high production in a short period of time. Since low-cost coal and nuclear plants can't ramp up quickly, more expensive gas-fired plants must cut in to do the job.

That change has a major impact on prices on the wholesale electricity market. Each owner who sends a unit of electricity into the bulk power system at a given time gets paid the same amount: the cost of producing a unit of electricity at the last plant that was turned on, thus the most expensive one. So when PVs come online, expensive gas-fired plants shut off, and the price paid to everyone drops. Then when the sun goes away and PV production abruptly disappears, gas-fired plants are turned back on and the price goes way up.

As a result, when PV systems are operating and PV penetrations are high, prices are low, and when they shut down, prices are high. Owners of PV systems thus receive the low prices and never the high. Moreover, their reimbursement declines as more solar power comes online.

Under current conditions, as more PV systems come online, reimbursements to solar owners will shrink to the point that investing in solar is no longer profitable at market prices. "So people may think that if solar power becomes very inexpensive, then everything will become solar," says Pérez-Arriaga. "But we find that that won't happen. There's a natural limit to solar penetration after which investment in more solar will not be economically viable."

Document 4

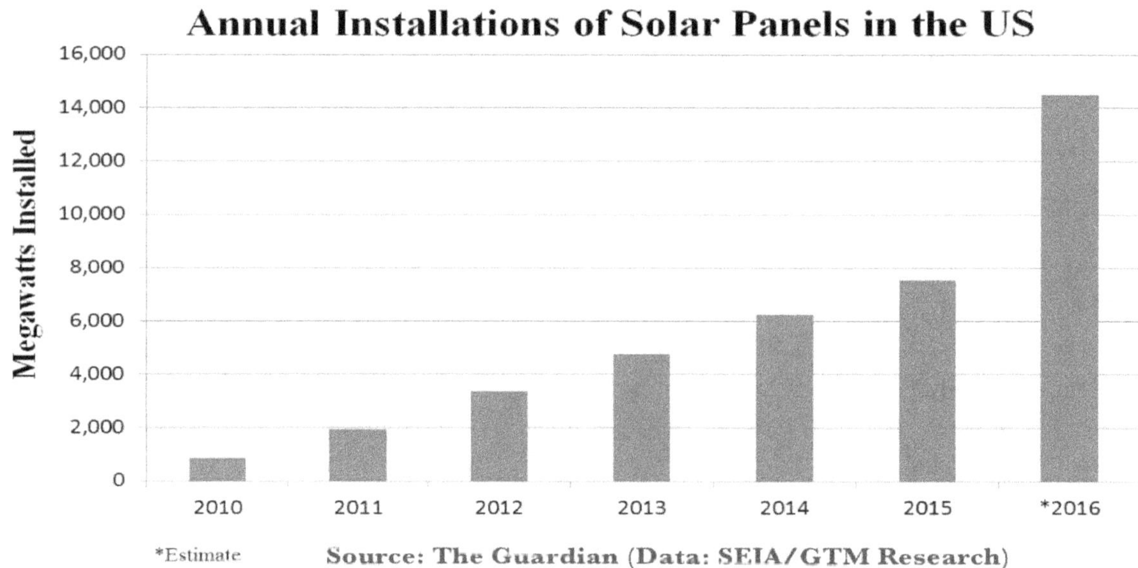

*Estimate   **Source: The Guardian (Data: SEIA/GTM Research)**

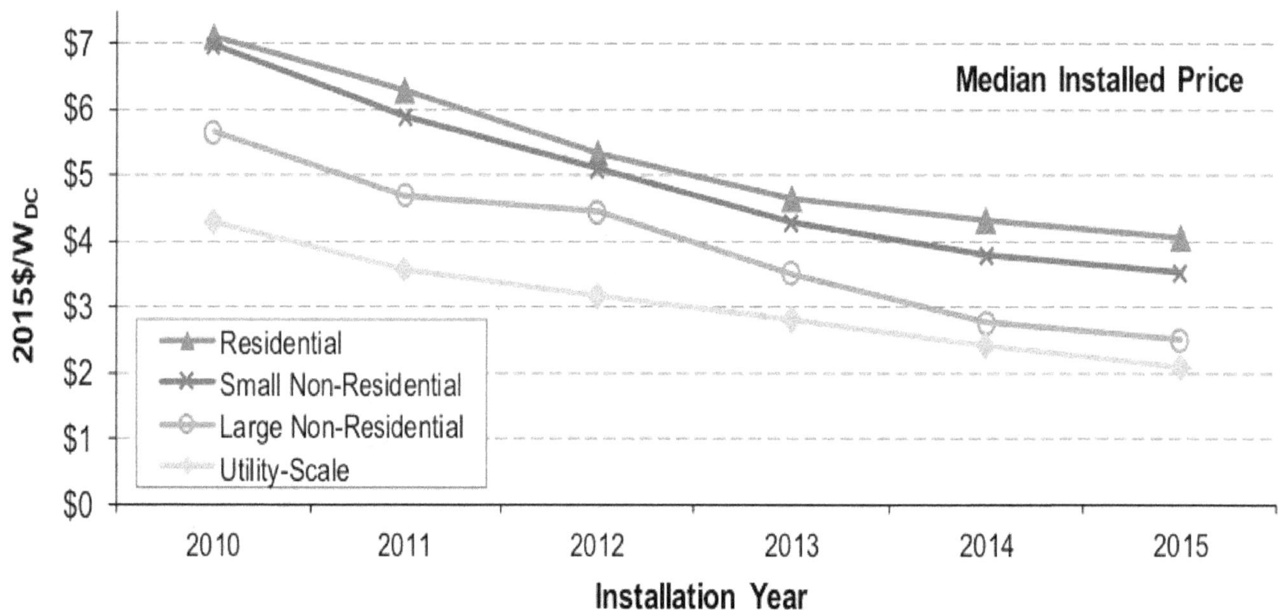

Cost per watt of solar installations in DC 2010-2015 – Source : The Scientific American

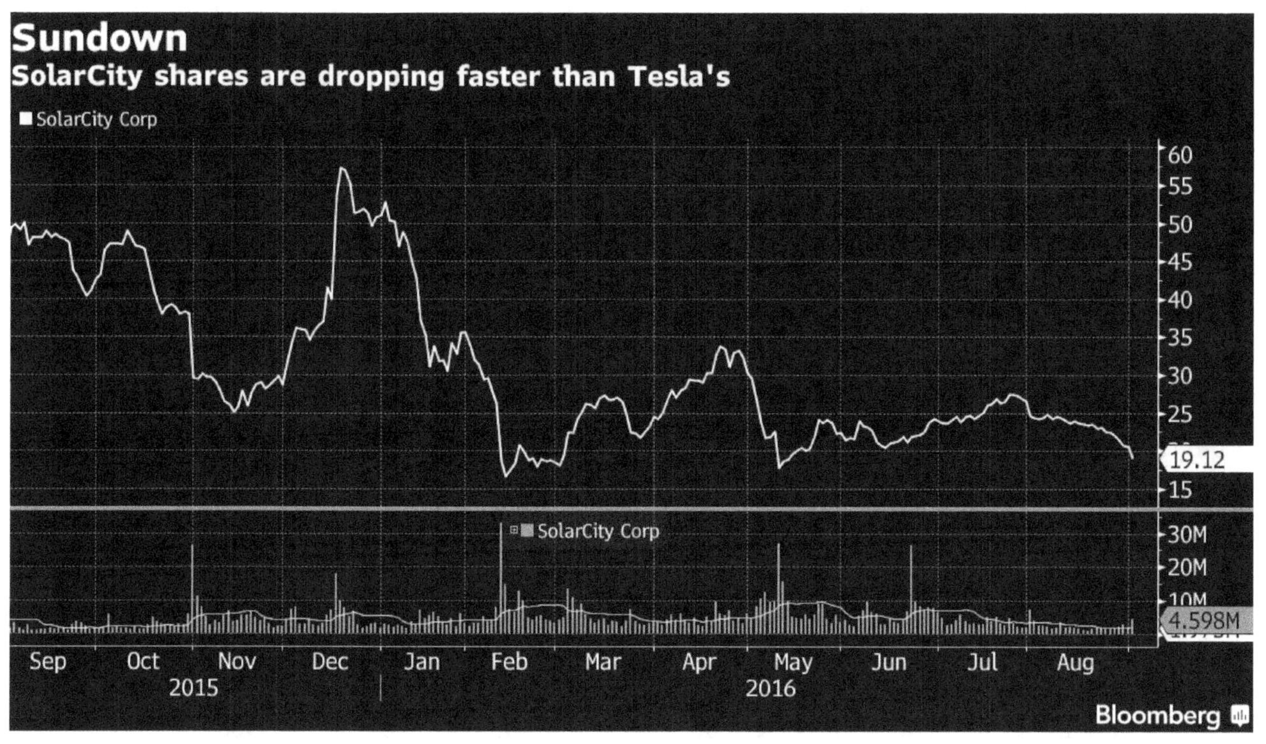

Sundown
SolarCity shares are dropping faster than Tesla's
SolarCity Corp
60
55
50
45
40
35
30
25
19.12
15
SolarCity Corp
30M
20M
10M
4.598M
Sep
Oct
2015
Nov
Dec
Jan
Feb
Mar
Apr
May
2016
Jun
Jul
Aug
Bloomberg

Sujet B – Document 5

Will Facebook and Elon Musk rewrite the myth of Icarus ?

Two Silicon Valley players are banking on the sun to free the world

Anna Wittwer – *Synthesis* - October 8, 2016

Last July Facebook successfully tested its solar-powered drone, code-named Aquila. If all goes according to plan, hundreds of these 400 kg hang-glider-like devices will soon be flying in circles at an altitude higher than jetliners, in order to provide internet access to deprived areas ; this could work thanks to a technology called Free Space Optics, which is roughly about laser beams. With its PV panels, Aquila can power itself, beam data to the surface, and be steered back to earth after a few months' operation. At this altitude insolation is permanent, except at night of course, but batteries store enough energy during the day to keep the machine in the air.

In the Greek myth, Icarus and his father Dedalus escaped from the labyrinth by attaching wings to their arms. Exhilarated by the experience, Icarus attempted to fly higher, closer to the sun, so that the wax that glued the feathers together melted and he fell into the sea.

It was the sun that precipitated the fall of Icarus ; but it is the sun that powers the flight of Aquila.

This incites me to approach recent moves by visionary entrepreneurs in the light of the myth and its reversal. The traditional interpretation of Icarus' fate is that Man, in his attempt to escape from the maze-like prison that human life is, creates artifices; but when these succeed, he may be tempted to overreach : Man wants to go too high, too far, too fast, and ignores the laws of nature that apply to him too. The retribution for this is a resounding crash.

I see some Silicon Valley players this year as very epic in their efforts to transcend the current limitations we face in achieving the energy transition ; one of them at least is doing it in a way that is « icaresque », ie both admirable and reckless. I am not thinking of Mark Zuckerberg, whose internet.org project to bring low-cost, reliable, carbon-free internet to the developing world is likely to succeed thanks to Aquila ;   my Icarus is Elon Musk, who may have overreached in his bid to create a synergy between Tesla motors and SolarCity, his struggling solar-home company. The sound of crash is already in his ears, as Wall Street balks at burning enormous amounts of cash in a venture with no short-term returns.

What is admirable ? It is the way both of these private initiatives are working to accelerate history and free the planet from fossil fuel use in the face of obstruction that can compare to gravity. Like Icarus', this is a story of liberation ; Facebook's Internet.org, however, is not reckless : the Aquila project has been wonderfully thought out. The craft should be relatively cheap to manufacture and maintain, re-usable, with virtually no carbon footprint. It is at the same time high-tech (FSO *is* high-tech) and low-tech enough to be operated and serviced anywhere in the world. It could deliver internet almost – if not entirely – free of charge for users in rural areas everywhere and zero-internet zones in Asia, Latin America and Africa. The hurdles Facebook is facing are rather political than financial or technical : it was recently criticized by the founder of the Internet, Tim Berners-Lee, on suspicions of snooping and because Aquila would violate net neutrality (IPs would initially provide only some services, including... Facebook).

Now Elon Musk, for his part, is battling something like the law of Newton in his attempt « to try to accelerate the advent of a sustainable-energy world.", as he described the merger to a shareholders meeting. He is up against the US electricity industry, nothing less. His bid rests on the hope of force-marching the US towards that tipping-point where renewable energy becomes irresistible. If his attempt succeeds and he really can get Tesla to develop those lithium-ion batteries to go with solar home packs manufactured and installed by SolarCity, this will be momentous : it means that your home, my home, your company, my company, can become self-reliant. We come off the grid. Local communities come off the grid. Many industries cut their petrol and gas bill. We refill our cars with the electricity from our roofs. Municipalities use public land to instal solar utilities to provide dirt-cheap power to people without roofs or gardens. Farewell, fossil fuel cars. So down also comes a big chunk of the energy sector.

No wonder Wall Street is in awe at the prospect of the merger. Its not only about the fresh mountains of cash that Musk is going to burn in the venture before any profit is made (on top of his dizzying debt) . It might also be because financiers are aware this is about backing a mighty game-changer.

If Facebook's Aquila literally reverses the myth of Icarus, it is very possible that Musk will reverse it too, in a more abstract manner : freeing us from fossil fuels, but also from economic and technical dependency on the energy sector. Moving us a little bit further from the capitalist model. Clean, *free* (or nearly free) energy for all (after the initial investment), wouldn't that be a huge leap forward in the real liberation to which we all aspire? If Musk succeeds, we may all fly closer to the sun. Let us hope Icarus makes it this time. (919 words)

SUJET CENTRALE-SUPÉLEC N° 1

(4 documents, synthèse 500 mots +/- 10 %)

Document 1

I Am Not Charlie Hebdo

David Brooks (1), *New York Times,* JAN. 8, 2015

The journalists at Charlie Hebdo are now rightly being celebrated as martyrs on behalf of freedom of expression, but let's face it: If they had tried to publish their satirical newspaper on any American university campus over the last two decades it wouldn't have lasted 30 seconds. Student and faculty groups would have accused them of hate speech. The administration would have cut financing and shut them down.

Public reaction to the attack in Paris has revealed that there are a lot of people who are quick to lionize (2) those who offend the views of Islamist terrorists in France but who are a lot less tolerant toward those who offend their own views at home.

Just look at all the people who have overreacted to campus micro-aggressions. The University of Illinois fired a professor who taught the Roman Catholic view on homosexuality. The University of Kansas suspended a professor for writing a harsh tweet against the N.R.A. Vanderbilt University derecognized (3) a Christian group that insisted that it *(= Vanderbilt University)* be led by Christians.

Americans may laud Charlie Hebdo for being brave enough to publish cartoons ridiculing the Prophet Muhammad, but, if Ayaan Hirsi Ali (4) is invited to campus, there are often calls to deny her a podium.

So this might be a teachable moment. As we are mortified by the slaughter of those writers and editors in Paris, it's a good time to come up with a less hypocritical approach to our own controversial figures, provocateurs and satirists.

The first thing to say, I suppose, is that whatever you might have put on your Facebook page yesterday, it is inaccurate for most of us to claim, Je Suis Charlie Hebdo, or I Am Charlie Hebdo. Most of us don't actually engage in the sort of deliberately offensive humor that that newspaper specializes in.

We might have started out that way. When you are 13, it seems daring and provocative to "épater la bourgeoisie," to stick a finger in the eye of authority, to ridicule other people's religious beliefs.

But after a while that seems puerile. Most of us move toward more complicated views of reality and more forgiving views of others. (Ridicule becomes less fun as you become more aware of your own frequent ridiculousness.) Most of us do try to show a modicum of respect for people of different creeds and faiths. We do try to open conversations with listening rather than insult.

Yet, at the same time, most of us know that provocateurs and other outlandish figures serve useful public roles. Satirists and ridiculers expose our weakness and vanity when we are feeling proud. They puncture the self-puffery of the successful. They level social inequality by bringing the mighty low. When they are effective they help us address our foibles communally, since laughter is one of the ultimate bonding experiences.

Moreover, provocateurs and ridiculers expose the stupidity of the fundamentalists. Fundamentalists are people who take everything literally. They are incapable of multiple viewpoints. They are incapable of seeing that while their religion may be worthy of the deepest reverence, it is also true that most religions are kind of weird. Satirists expose those who are incapable of laughing at themselves and teach the rest of us that we probably should.

In short, in thinking about provocateurs and insulters, we want to maintain standards of civility and respect while at the same time allowing room for those creative and challenging folks who are uninhibited by good manners and taste.

If you try to pull off this delicate balance with law, speech codes and banned speakers, you'll end up with crude censorship and a strangled conversation. It's almost always wrong to try to suppress speech, erect speech codes and disinvite speakers.

Fortunately, social manners are more malleable and supple than laws and codes. Most societies have successfully maintained standards of civility and respect while keeping open avenues for those who are funny, uncivil and offensive.

In most societies, there's the adults' table and there's the kids' table. The people who read *Le Monde* or the establishment organs are at the adults' table. The jesters, the holy fools and people like Ann Coulter and Bill Maher (5) are at the kids' table. They're not granted complete respectability, but they are heard because in their unguided missile manner, they sometimes say necessary things that no one else is saying.

Healthy societies, in other words, don't suppress speech, but they do grant different standing to different sorts of people. Wise and considerate scholars are heard with high respect. Satirists are heard with bemused semirespect. Racists and anti-Semites are heard through a filter of opprobrium and disrespect. People who want to be heard attentively have to earn it through their conduct.

The massacre at Charlie Hebdo should be an occasion to end speech codes. And it should remind us to be legally tolerant toward offensive voices, even as we are socially discriminating.**(823)**

1. David Brooks is a « pundit », a highly-regarded American conservative political and cultural commentator who has been writing for *The New York Times* since 2003. He represents the conservative voice of the NY Times, which by and large is a liberal paper, in conformity with the American tradition of plurality of opinions in the media. His clever, non-partisan, knowledgeable and distanced editorials have long commanded respect. A very good read for students.

2. To lionize : to give a lot of public attention and approval to (someone); to treat as a celebrity

3. to derecognize : to remove official recognition, approval or authorization

4. Ayaan Hirsi Ali is a Somali-born American (formerly Dutch) activist, writer, and politician. She is known for her views critical of female genital mutilation and Islam and supportive of women's rights and atheism. (source : wikipedia)

5. Ann Hart Coulter est une commentatrice politique, auteur de best-sellers, conférencière et polémiste républicaine aux États-Unis. Connue pour son style controversé et ses idées conservatrices, elle a été souvent décrite comme « la Michael Moore du Parti Républicain ». Ann Coulter se définit comme un auteur polémique et engagé qui aime bien donner des coups de pied dans la fourmilière et ne prétend pas être neutre ou impartiale. Elle se distingue par son acrimonie envers le Parti démocrate et la gauche . Bill Maher, quant à lui, est un humoriste, animateur de télévision et commentateur politique américain connu pour ses prises de position polémiques dans un pays où, selon lui, règnent depuis les années 1980 à la fois un certain conformisme et un profond individualisme au sens sociologique. Les thèmes qu'il aborde touchent à la politique, l'économie, la religion ou la société.

http://www.nytimes.com/2015/01/09/opinion/david-brooks-i-am-not-charlie-hebdo.html?_r=0

Document 2

George Orwell's Proposed Preface to 'Animal Farm' - 1945

(...)Unpopular ideas can be silenced, and inconvenient facts kept dark, without the need for any official ban. Anyone who has lived long in a foreign country will know of instances of sensational items of news — things which on their own merits would get the big headlines – being kept right out of the British press, not because the Government intervened but because of a general tacit agreement that 'it wouldn't do' to mention that particular fact. So far as the daily newspapers go, this is easy to understand. The British press is extremely centralised, and most of it is owned by wealthy men who have every motive to be dishonest on certain important topics. But the same kind of veiled censorship also operates in books and periodicals, as well as in plays, films and radio. At any given moment there is an orthodoxy, a body of ideas which it is assumed that all right-thinking people will accept without question. It is not exactly forbidden to say this, that or the other, but it is 'not done' to say it(...)

At this moment what is demanded by the prevailing orthodoxy is an uncritical admiration of Soviet Russia. Everyone knows this, nearly everyone acts on it. Any serious criticism of the Soviet régime, any disclosure of facts which the Soviet government would prefer to keep hidden, is next door to unprintable. And this nation-wide conspiracy to flatter our ally takes place, curiously enough, against a background of genuine intellectual tolerance. For though you are not allowed to criticise the Soviet government, at least you are reasonably free to criticise our own. (...) So long as the prestige of the USSR is not involved, the principle of free speech has been reasonably well upheld.

(…) The issue involved here is quite a simple one: Is every opinion, however unpopular — however foolish, even — entitled to a hearing? Put it in that form and nearly any English intellectual will feel that he ought to say 'Yes'. But give it a concrete shape, and ask, 'How about an attack on Stalin? Is *that* entitled to a hearing?', and the answer more often than not will be 'No'. In that case the current orthodoxy happens to be challenged, and so the principle of free speech lapses. Now, when one demands liberty of speech and of the press, one is not demanding absolute liberty. There always must be, or at any rate there always will be, some degree of censorship, so long as organised societies endure. But freedom, as Rosa Luxembourg [*sic*] said, is 'freedom for the other fellow'. The same principle is contained in the famous words of Voltaire: 'I detest what you say; I will defend to the death your right to say it.' If the intellectual liberty which without a doubt has been one of the distinguishing marks of western civilisation means anything at all, it means that everyone shall have the right to say and to print what he believes to be the truth, provided only that it does not harm the rest of the community in some quite unmistakable way. Both capitalist democracy and the western versions of Socialism have till recently taken that principle for granted. Our Government, as I have already pointed out, still makes some show of respecting it. The ordinary people in the street-partly, perhaps, because they are not sufficiently interested in ideas to be intolerant about them - still vaguely hold that 'I suppose everyone's got a right to their own opinion.' It is only, or at any rate it is chiefly, the literary and scientific intelligentsia, the very people who ought to be the guardians of liberty, who are beginning to despise it, in theory as well as in practice.

These people don't see that if you encourage totalitarian methods, the time may come when they will be used against you instead of for you. Make a habit of imprisoning Fascists without trial, and perhaps the process won't stop at Fascists. (...) Tolerance and decency are deeply rooted in England, but they are not indestructible, and they have to be kept alive partly by conscious effort. The result of preaching totalitarian doctrines is to weaken the instinct by means of which free peoples know what is or is not dangerous. (...)

It is important to realise that the current Russomania is only a symptom of the general weakening of the western liberal tradition. Had the MOI(1) chipped in and definitely vetoed the publication of this book, the bulk of the English intelligentsia would have seen nothing disquieting in this. Uncritical loyalty to the USSR happens to be the current orthodoxy, and where the supposed interests of the USSR are involved they are willing to tolerate not only censorship but the deliberate falsification of history. (...) Quite possibly that particular fashion will not last. For all I know, by the time this book is published my view of the Soviet régime may be the generally-accepted one. But what use would that be in itself? To exchange one orthodoxy for another is not necessarily an advance. The enemy is the gramophone mind, whether or not one agrees with the record that is being played at the moment.

I am well acquainted with all the arguments against freedom of thought and speech — the arguments which claim that it cannot exist, and the arguments which claim that it ought not to. I answer simply that they don't convince me and that our civilisation over a period of four hundred years has been founded on the opposite notice. For quite a decade past I have believed that the existing Russian régime is a mainly evil thing, and I claim the right to say so, in spite of the fact that we are allies with the USSR in a war which I want to see won. If I had to choose a text to justify myself, I should choose the line from Milton:

By the known rules of ancient liberty.

The word 'ancient' emphasises the fact that intellectual freedom is a deep-rooted tradition without which our characteristic western culture could only doubtfully exist. From that tradition many of our intellectuals are visibly turning away. They have accepted the principle that a book should be published or suppressed, praised or damned, not on its merits but according to political expediency. And others who do not actually hold this view assent to it from sheer cowardice. (...) I know that the English intelligentsia have plenty of reason for their timidity and dishonesty, indeed I know by heart the arguments by which they justify themselves. But at least let us have no more nonsense about defending liberty against Fascism. If liberty means anything at all it means the right to tell people what they do not want to hear.(...) (1132)

(1) Ministry of the Interior (which indirectly let Orwell know it was unreasonable to publish his satire of the Soviet regime in 1945)

Document 3

We've created a world of touchy fools

Howard Jacobson – *The Independent* – October 30, 2015

(…) Our country is in a censorious mood. The more educated we are, the less we are prepared to tolerate views contrary to our own. Shake any institution of higher learning and a dozen boycotters will fall out of it. If the academic community gets its way, we will soon all be speaking with a single voice.

But it isn't just the desire to silence dissenting opinion that should worry us. Let us say that Greer (1) didn't just happen to think differently from those she has distressed but intended, for whatever reason – because she's Australian, say – to go out of her way to needle them. Why, even then, should she be denied the right to a platform?

It isn't only in the name of free speech that the views of an itchy polemicist should be tolerated – and I say itchy polemicist promoting thought, not itchy ideologue promoting violence – but because provocation is indispensable to the workings of a sound, creative culture. The loser, when silencers have their way, is not the provocateur but the provoked. To be easily offended is to be shut off from the invigoration of that argumentative give-and-take we call liberty; not to understand the poetics of provocation is to miss out on the joys of living in a literate and robust society that excels at satire and burlesque.

We hear too much of "phobia". Attach "phobia" to any cause you care for and you have ring-fenced it against the words of the critic and the devious antics of the clown alike. Nothing is to be mocked; everything – except the act of critical dissent itself – is sacrosanct. Thus have we created for ourselves an impoverished world of touchy fools who understand no mode of address other than the internet's yes/no, like/dislike, thumbs up/thumbs down discourse of the dumb.

Take some of the responses to Martin Amis's splenetic and self-consciously snobby dismantling of Jeremy Corbyn in The Sunday Times last week (2). That the straight-faced of social media were going to throw a blue fit over this would assuredly have entered Amis's calculations. It can be fun for a writer with a comic gift to drive the over-principled into an apoplexy. That's part of what a comic gift is for. "Dance," says Martin Amis, and true to expectation, they dance their hobbled dance, outraged by his ridicule, sickened by the position of educational privilege from which he mocks Corbyn's intellectual penury, primly unamused by the unashamedly ad hominem nature of his attack. (No matter that with Jeremy Corbyn – a man admired for nothing more substantial than "authenticity" – ad hominem is all there is.)

(...)As for snobbish derision, it is of noble ancestry, going back to Hamlet twitting Polonius, Pope, Swift, Wilde, Waugh: a line of scurrilous mirth whose slithering ambiguities make a Charlie of whoever can't keep up. Equivocation is at the heart of literary insult, harnessing seriousness to comedy, earnestness to lightness, teasing the single-minded into taking offence. Sadistic? Yes, but then again no.

The impulse to irresponsible play is lost on the easily provoked who think a writer must mean what he appears to mean, say what he seems to say, or indeed say anything, because saying, reader, is the least of what a writer does.

Half the time, if it's any good, writing is a wind-up, a trap for the unwary. To be wound up in the playground was always a humiliation; to be wound up on the page is no different. We must get off our high horses. We look stupid up there. (597 words)

(1) In 2015 iconic 1960s feminist Germaine Greer made a very controversial statement about transgender people, which offended the LGBT community

Document 4

Cartoon by Gee, January 9, 2015

SUJET CENTRALE-SUPÉLEC N° 2

(4 documents, synthèse 500 mots +/- 10 %)

Document 1

Nick Hornby, Introduction to *Fever Pitch* (1)

SUNDAY, 14TH JULY 1991

It's in there all the time, looking for a way out.

I wake up around ten, make two cups of tea, take them into the bedroom, place one on each side of the bed. Wc both sip thoughtfully ; so soon after waking there are long, dream-filled gaps between the occasional remarks – about the rain outside, about last night, about smoking in the bedroom when I have agreed not to. She asks what I'm doing this week, and I think : (1) I'm seeing Matthew on Wednesday. (2) Matthew's still got my *Champions* video. (3) {*Remembering that Matthew, a purely nominal Arsenal fan, has not been to Highbury for a couple of years, and so has had no opportunity to watch more recent recruits in the flesh*} I wonder what he thought of Anders Limpar.

And in three easy stages, within fifteen, twenty minutes of waking, I'm on my way. I see Limpar running at Gillespie, swaying to his right, going down : PENALTY ! DIXON SCORES ! 2— 0 !... Merson's back-heel flick and Smith's right-foot shot into the far corner in the same match... Merson's little push past Grobbelaar up at Anfield... Davis's swivel and smash against Villa... (And this, remember, is a morning in July, our month off, when there is no club football of any kind.) Sometimes, when I let this dreamy state take me over completely, I go on and back, through Anfield '89, Wembley '87, Stamford Bridge '78, my whole footballing life flashing before my eyes.

'What are you thinking about ?' she asks.

At this point I lie. I wasn't thinking about Martin Amis or Gérard Depardieu or the Labour Party at all. But then, obsessives have no choice ; they have to lie on occasions like this. If we told the truth every time, then we would be unable to maintain relationships with anyone from the real world. We would be left to rot with our arsenal programmes or our collection of original blue-label Stax records or our King Charles spaniels, and our two-minute daydreams would become longer and longer and longer until we lost our jobs and stopped bathing and shaving and eating, and we would lie on the floor in our own filth rewinding the video again and again in an attempt to memorise by heart the *whole* of the commentary, including David Pleat's expert analysis, for the night of 26th of May 1989. (You think I had to look the date up ? Ha!) The truth is : *for alarmingly large chunks of an average day, I am a moron.*

I would not wish to suggest that the contemplation of football is in itself an improper use of the imagination. David Lacey, the chief football correspondent for the *Guardian*, is a fine writer and an obviously intelligent man, and presumably he must devote even more of his interior life than I do to the game. The difference between Lacey and me is that I rarely *think*. I remember, I fantasise, I try to visualise every one of Alan Smith's goals, I tick off the number of First Division grounds I have visited ; once or twice, when I have been unable to sleep, I have tried to count the names of the wives and girlfriends of the Double-winning team ; now, I can only remember that Charlie George's fiancée was called Susan Farge, and that Bob Wilson's wife was called Megs, but even this partial recall is terrifyingly unnecessary.)

None of this is thought, in the proper sense of the word. There is no analysis, or self-awareness, or mental rigour going on at all, because obsessives are denied any kind of perspective on their own passion. This, in a sense, is what defines an obsessive (and serves to explain why so few of them recognize themselves as such.

(...)*Fever Pitch* is an attempt to gain some kind of angle on my obsession. Why has the relationship that began as a schoolboy crush endured for nearly a quarter of a century, longer than any other relationship I have made of my own free will ?

(...)This book is also, in part, an exploration of some of the meanings that football seems to contain for many of us. It has become quite clear to me that my devotion says things about my own character and personal history, but the way the game is consumed seems to offer all sorts of information about our society and culture. (I have friends who will regard this as pretentious, self-serving nonsense, the kind of desperate justification one might expect from a man who has spent a huge chunk of his leisure time fretting miserably in the cold. They are particularly resistant to the idea because I tend to overestimate the metaphorical value of football, and therefore introduce it into conversations where it simply does not belong. I now accept that football has no relevance to the Falklands conflict, the Rushdie affair, the Gulf War, childbirth, the ozone layer, the poll tax, etc., etc. , and I would like to apologise to anyone who has had to listen to my pathetically strained analogies.)

Finally, *Fever Pitch* is about being a fan. I have read books written by people who obviously love football, but that's a different thing entirely ; and I have read books written, for want of a better word, by hooligans, but at least 95 per cent of the millions who watch games every year have never hit anyone in their lives. So this is for the rest of us, and for anyone who has wondered what it might be like to be this way. While the details are unique to me, I hope that they will strike a chord with anyone who has ever found themselves drifting off, in the middle of a working day or a film or a conversation, towards a left-foot volley into a top right-hand corner ten or fifteen or twenty-five years ago. (994 words)

(1) British award-winning writer Nick Hornby's largely autobiographical novel Fever Pitch was published in 1991 to critical acclaim.

Document 2

Ed Smith – The New Statesman - 3 December 2015

Naivety is usually considered a disastrous quality in a leader. Impatient ruthlessness, the feint to the media, the knowing wink: Machiavellianism dominates conventional wisdom about how winners operate. Too much so. Naivety is underrated, especially as an influence over long-term success.

"Make this the greatest football club in the world within 100 years" – that was the message given to Arsène Wenger by the chairman of the Japanese club Nagoya Grampus Eight when the Frenchman became its manager in 1995. "That negates the pressure of immediacy in a fabulous way," Wenger reflected recently in a fascinating interview in L'Équipe.

Arsenal fans may wonder if the 100-year coaching term lodged permanently in Wenger's mind. He has now been manager of Arsenal for more than 7,000 days, longer than all current Premier League managers put together. The League titles have dried up, yet the body of achievement grows.

Wenger's naivety can hurt him and Arsenal. His lack of tactical savvy costs games, especially when he refuses to substitute underperforming players. Concerns about their long-term self-esteem blind him to the danger on the left flank right now. Wenger is not ruthless. Players seem not to fear his vengeance. He appears coolly rational but suffers from a surfeit of forgiveness, lacking Graham Greene's "chip of ice" in his heart.

This makes him frustrating. But Wenger's naivety also drives his long-term success. His players do not burn out from psychological duress (a common explanation of José Mourinho's short stints in charge of clubs: the players can't take it any more). Real teachers are always optimists and Wenger's central interest, improving his players, does not pall or weary.

He is often described as a "developmental manager", as though that quality leads him to be a limited and indulgent tactician. We might reverse the causality: being a tolerant, light-touch tactician sustains his gift as a long-term educator. To expect more of people and risk being let down can be an effective style of long-range leadership.

(...)The experience of watching sport, like that of reading a book, can be downgraded retrospectively. Looking back, it is possible to feel, if not exactly tricked, then sceptical about the emotions we imagined during it. The passing of time enhances some sporting - experiences and diminishes others.

How will Wenger be remembered? We will look back on a stubborn idealist with huge blind spots (central defenders, goalkeepers, defensive midfielders, and so on). But I predict that the experience of following Wenger's Arsenal will take on even more depth and value in retrospect.

What is success in sport? Matches won, titles acquired, cabinets stocked? That's true but only up to a point. The rival view, holding that sport is entertainment, is also highly incomplete: if you want only to entertain, you are a clown not a sportsman; if you seek beauty alone, you are a dancer. The ultimate trick is holding the two values – victory and entertainment – in perfect equipoise.

The greatest champions are alive to the additional expectations of entertainment without allowing it to interfere. Those players (and teams) are open to the way that sport is about more than winning without becoming significantly less likely to win. The crowd understands this: fans do not crave indulgence, like a child needing to be tickled, but respect. That bond between players and spectators, however, must stay one step removed from the task at hand.

In its highest form, sport is never less than entertaining but always more than entertainment. And that has been central to the experience of following Arsenal these past 19 years. Forget style and finesse for a moment. The real joy has been justified hope, the sense of having a chance – even if the hope does not materialise. It is adolescent to believe that winning is the only pleasure in sport. If I lose myself in a match, following the narrative surprises all the way to the final whistle, surely I have had a successful experience?

That has been Wenger's gift, given to Arsenal and to English football for nearly two decades. When Mourinho described Wenger as "a specialist in failure", it was not cruelly accurate but sadly false. It showed the limitations of Mourinho's world-view.

I have enough reverence for talent and achievement to expect Mourinho to prove his critics wrong. But, over the long term, don't bet against Wenger having the last laugh. Naive hopefulness is strangely enduring. I hope, however, that it doesn't take 100 years for Wenger to be proved right. (751 words)

Read full article here :http://www.newstatesman.com/politics/sport/2015/12/mourinho-tactician-and-wenger-educator-both-are-perfectionists-just-different

DOCUMENT 3

Why Americans (Rightly) Hate Soccer

Stephen Moore – The Daily Signal (1)– June 26th, 2014

The World Cup is underway, and other than the Olympics, it will surely be the most closely followed sporting event with estimates of more than one billion TV viewers worldwide.

Oh, and I won't be one of them.

Why?

Soccer is B-O-R-I-N-G.

I've often argued that in the entire world, the only thing worse than playing soccer is watching it. It's about as exciting as staring at the clothes dryer for two hours as your shirts and pants tumble around.

Just as in soccer, if you go to get a sandwich or go for a mile walk and then return to the screen, guess what? Nothing has happened.

The last soccer match I watched was when the U.S. women played China for the championship and after what seemed like an eternity – consecutive life sentences – the score was zero to zero.That was scintillating. Now let's really get wild and watch a congressional hearing on CSPAN(2).

Every soccer match is like watching a North Carolina basketball game before the shot clock(3) when Dean Smith invented the four corner offense.

I've often said that after having to watch my three sons play junior soccer, now I know why Europeans riot at soccer matches. For the same reason that inmates riot in prisons: there's nothing else to do. It's good exercise for sure, but to what end? If golf is a good walk spoiled, then soccer is a good run spoiled.

And what is with the ugly polyester soccer uniforms?

I'm an American. I want scoring. I want action. Maybe it's part of the instant gratification culture but 90 minutes of kicking with zero or one or two goals doesn't exactly move heaven and earth.

And because scoring is such a lightning striking rarity, once a team gets up by two or three goals, turn the lights out, it's like being down 49-0 in football. In other words, soccer lacks one of the best parts of watching a sport: the comeback. It almost never happens. If a team gets up by three goals they might as well invoke the slaughter rule.

Because scoring is so nearly impossible, many of the matches come down to faking a penalty (flopping) in order to get a penalty kick. The referees are the most important people on the field.So the key to being a good soccer player is to be a really good actor.

I've also argued that soccer is a manifestation of the labor theory of value applied to sports—which may explain why socialist European nations do so well.

Soccer is a huge expenditure of human effort and exertion with almost no return. Under capitalism the idea is to produce the most output with the least amount of work. Because there is so little scoring and so little of the action bears on the outcome of the game, every crazed soccer mom can convince their child that they are above average.

Here we are in America, the world's economic and military superpower, and the richest place on the planet. Yet the odds of America winning the Cup this year are 100-1. We're like Fairleigh Dickinson going up against Kentucky in the NCAA basketball tournament.

Now basketball, that's real action. And we are indisputably the world superpower in that sport.

Or let's have a World Cup tournament in "football" on the gridiron(4). Given the lousy state of the economy, the ISIS offensives in Iraq, and a White House that seems to be fighting a new scandal every 24 hours, America needs a lift.

The World Cup surely isn't it – we will leave that to Germany and Brazil.(607)

(1)The Daily Signal is the multimedia news organization of The Heritage Foundation, an ultra-conservative American think-tank. This op-ed was first published on Fox News.
(2) C-SPAN retransmet, entre autres affaires publiques, les débats parlementaires.

(3) time limit to score

(4) = a tournament of American football

DOCUMENT 4

Source: various Manchester United fan sites on the internet

SUJET CENTRALE-SUPÉLEC N° 3

(4 documents, synthèse 500 mots +/- 10 %)

DOCUMENT 1

Tech fatigue

Posted Apr 19, 2016 by Romain Dillet (@romaindillet) - TechCrunch.com

This isn't a rant post. But if you have worked in tech for long enough, you know this feeling — tech fatigue. At some point, everything new feels old, everything different feels dumb. If you get stuck in this circle of endless cynicism, you need to ask yourself the important questions.

First, let me tell you how I feel about tech today. Everything feels derivative or silly. I've been there before, I've seen that. Tech companies are churning out new products that look like last year's products, media outlets are giving me a *déjà-vu* and the current new trends have been the same trends for the past two years.

A pink MacBook sounds anything but new. Slack is turning into Yammer (1)— time to party like it's 2012. Apparently, I need to update my USB Type C adapter now. And Snapchat is becoming more like Messenger is becoming more like WeChat, proving that at some point messaging apps are going to be derivative products of all other messaging apps.

But it's fine, you think, I just have to look at the future. So let's head to Las Vegas. Another CES (2), and this time I bump into Walt Mossberg (3). I ask him how many times he's been to CES. The number was so high that I forgot what it was. He's counting in decades, not years. He was even in Las Vegas before CES was called CES. I probably have baby tech fatigue compared to him.

So what does the future look like? We've been talking about virtual reality, artificial intelligence and self-driving cars for years already. Now these trends sound like random buzzwords more than anything else. Remember when the next big thing was supposed to be Meerkat live streams, Foursquare checkins and 3D printing?

(...)The next day, other tech reporters ask me if I think augmented reality is more relevant than virtual reality. All I can think about is all the useless connected objects around me. I'm thinking about making a Gmail filter that auto-forwards stupid pitches(4) to @internetofshit.(...)More recently, I attended another big Netflix press conference with no apparent reason, another tech event with a bunch of new faces. I wondered whether it was time to rage-quit tech and work in the fashion industry. *(attention saut de page technique, le texte continue plus bas)*

All of this culminated into my mood today.

(...)Tech fatigue is a good thing if you know what to do with it. And the reason why this post isn't a rant is that I'm still optimistic about tech. There are just some conditions.

In 2012, shortly after John Biggs hired me, then TechCrunch co-editor Alexia Tsotsis asked me a serious question — why do you care about tech?

At the time, I didn't have a good answer. But when tech fatigue hits you, it's important to ask yourself this question again — and refine your answer.

I care about tech for two simple reasons. First, technology is incredibly powerful and can profoundly alter how we communicate, share information and learn. It has brought people, things and services together that couldn't be brought together before. Tech has drastically improved productivity, created many jobs (for now) and, more importantly, reduced inequalities — at least for those who get access to these devices and services.

Tech companies have an indirect effect on billions of people. While most people aren't directly better off thanks to Facebook, Google, Apple and Microsoft, the evolution of computers and the Internet is the most important technological revolution of our lifetime. It affects the structure of our societies. Sure, there are unfortunate side effects, and governments will have to make sure tech companies don't get too powerful. But I believe tech is slowly but surely improving the lives of many, many people.

Second, the tech industry is a fascinating industry. I'm very fortunate that I love my job. Sure, the news cycles can be tiring sometimes. But I get to talk to smart people every day. I get to talk about the future with them. And I get to help those who have great ideas and need an audience. I also believe sharing knowledge about the tech industry is an important mission.

Uncovering the next big thing before most people is exciting as well. And TechCrunch is the best megaphone to do this. Thinking that I have this unique opportunity to contribute to the public debate around tech is invaluable. I'm incredibly lucky.

These seem like simple reasons, but they are the reasons why I wake up every day. Now that I know why I care about tech, it makes tech fatigue much easier to understand. Tech fatigue is a signal. Tech fatigue tells me that I have to challenge myself every day to find new things. If I get stuck talking about the same trends and products, I'm missing out on what's going to make tech great tomorrow.

Second, tech fatigue is a great bullshit indicator. If something feels dumb, it's probably dumb. But it's my responsibility to find interesting things. Every day, an interesting new startup is created. So it's time to step out of my comfort zone and foster my curiosity, otherwise I'll just become a cranky old man.

And if you suffer from tech fatigue yourself, think about this as well — why do you like tech in the first place? And remember that everything new is already old, and everything unfamiliar is new.(897)

(1) Slack and Yammer are chat apps used mostly by employees at work

(2) Consumer Electronics Show, one of the biggest trade fairs in the world for that sector

(3) Walter S. Mossberg (born March 27, 1947) is an American journalist who was, from 1991 through 2013, the principal technology columnist for The Wall Street Journal.

(4) *Pitch* : ici, à prendre au sens de « projet » ou « innovation »

Read the full article here : *https://techcrunch.com/2016/04/19/tech-fatigue/*

Document 2

THE MURDERER, A short story by Ray Bradbury (1953) (edited)

"I'm here to help you," said the psychiatrist, frowning. Something was wrong with the room. He had hesitated the moment he entered. He glanced around. The prisoner laughed. "If you're wondering why it's so quiet in here, I just kicked the radio to death."

Violent, thought the doctor.

The prisoner read this thought, smiled, put out a gentle hand. "No, only to machines that yak-yak-yak."

Bits of the wall radio's tubes and wires lay on the gray carpeting. Ignoring these, feeling that smile upon him like a heat lamp, the psychiatrist sat across from his patient in the unusual silence which was like the gathering of a storm.

"You're Mr. Albert Brock, who calls himself The Murderer?"

Brock nodded pleasantly. "Before we start . . ." He moved quietly and quickly to detach the wrist radio from the doctor's arm. He tucked it in his teeth like a walnut, gritted, heard it crack, handed it back to the appalled psychiatrist as if he had done them both a favor. "That's better."

The psychiatrist stared at the ruined machine. "You're running up quite a damage bill."

"I don't care," smiled the patient. "As the old song goes: 'Don't Care What Happens to Me!' " He hummed it.

The psychiatrist said: "Shall we start?"

"Fine. The first victim, or one of the first, was my telephone. Murder most foul. I shoved it in the kitchen Insinkerator! Stopped the disposal unit in mid-swallow. Poor thing strangled to death. After that I shot the television set!"

The psychiatrist said, "Mmm."

"Fired six shots right through the cathode. Made a beautiful tinkling crash, like a dropped chandelier."

"Nice imagery."

"Thanks, I always dreamt of being a writer."

"Suppose you tell me when you first began to hate the telephone."

"It frightened me as a child. Uncle of mine called it the Ghost Machine. Voices without bodies. Scared the living hell out of me. Later in life I was never comfortable. Seemed to me a phone was an impersonal instrument. If it felt like it, it let your personality go through its wires. If it didn't want to, it just drained your personality away until what slipped through at the other end was some cold fish of a voice, all steel, copper, plastic, no warmth, no reality. It's easy to say the wrong thing on telephones; the telephone changes your meaning on you. First thing you know, you've made an enemy. Then, of course, the telephone's such a convenient thing; it just sits there and demands you call someone who doesn't want to be called. Friends were always calling, calling, calling me. Hell, I hadn't any time of my own. When it wasn't the telephone it was the television, the radio, the phonograph. When it wasn't the television or radio or the phonograph it was motion pictures at the corner theater, motion pictures projected, with commercials on low-lying cumulus clouds. It doesn't rain rain any more, it rains soapsuds. When it wasn't High-Fly Cloud advertisements, it was music by Mozzek in every restaurant; music and commercials on the busses I rode to work. When it wasn't music, it was interoffice communications, and my horror chamber of a radio wristwatch on which my friends and my wife phoned every five minutes. What is there about such 'conveniences' that makes them so temptingly convenient? The average man thinks, Here I am, time on my hands, and there on my wrist is a wrist telephone, so why not just buzz old Joe up, eh? 'Hello, hello!' I love my friends, my wife, humanity, very much, but when one minute my wife calls to say, 'Where are you now, dear?' and a friend calls and says, 'Got the best off-color joke to tell you. Seems there was a guy-' And a stranger calls and cries out, 'This is the Find-Fax Poll. What gum are you chewing at this very instant?' Well!"

"How did you feel during the week?"

"The fuse lit. On the edge of the cliff. That same afternoon I did what I did at the office."

"Which was?"

"I poured a paper cup of water into the intercommunications system."

The psychiatrist wrote on his pad.

"And the system shorted?"

"Beautifully! The Fourth of July on wheels! My God, stenographers ran around looking lost! What an uproar!"

"Felt better temporarily, eh?"

"Fine! Then I got the idea at noon of stomping my wrist radio on the sidewalk. A shrill voice was just yelling out of it at me, 'This is People's Poll Number Nine. What did you eat for lunch?' when I kicked the wrist radio!"

"Felt even better, eh?"

"It grew on me!" Brock rubbed his hands together. "Why didn't I start a solitary revolution, deliver man from certain 'conveniences'? 'Convenient for who?' I cried. Convenient for friends:

'Hey, Al, thought I'd call you from the locker room out here at Green Hills. Just made a sockdolager hole in one! A hole in one, Al! A beautiful day. Having a shot of whiskey now. Thought you'd want to know, Al!' Convenient for my office, so when I'm in the field with my radio car there's no moment when I'm not in touch. In touch! There's a slimy phrase. Touch, hell. Gripped! Pawed, rather. Mauled and massaged and pounded by FM voices. You can't leave your car without checking in: 'Have stopped to visit gas-station men's room.' 'Okay, Brock, step on it!' 'Brock, what took you so long?' 'Sorry, sir.' 'Watch it next time, Brock.' 'Yes, sir!' So, do you know what I did, Doctor? I bought a quart of French chocolate ice cream and spooned it into the car radio transmitter."

"Was there any special reason for selecting French chocolate ice cream to spoon into the broadcasting unit?"

Brock thought about it and smiled. "It's my favorite flavor."

"Oh," said the doctor.

"I figured, hell, what's good enough for me is good enough for the radio transmitter."

"What made you think of spooning ice cream into the radio?"

"It was a hot day."

The doctor paused.

"And what happened next?"

"Silence happened next. God, it was beautiful. That car radio cackling all day, 'Brock go here, Brock go there, Brock check in, Brock check out, okay Brock, hour lunch, Brock, lunch over, Brock, Brock, Brock.' Well, that silence was like putting ice cream in my ears."

"You seem to like ice cream a lot."

"I just rode around feeling of the silence. It's a big bolt of the nicest, softest flannel ever made. Silence. A whole hour of it. I just sat in my car, smiling, feeling of that flannel with my ears. I felt drunk with Freedom!" (...)

Read the full story here :

http://www.sediment.uni-goettingen.de/staff/dunkl/zips/The-Murderer.pdf

Document 3

Don't think you're superior to me because you're not on Facebook

Suzanne Moore – The Guardian - November 11, 2015

(...)All media is social media and everyone is a critic. We live in constant TripAdvisor mode. I am a hotel that did not impress you much. I am the Uber driver you only gave two stars to. I am a waste of space that you could not even be bothered to read, simply to slag off. Because there is no comment without comment. If a column is not retweeted does it even exist?

If I want "real life" I pull back from Twitter(...) and I go on Facebook. As Twitter's growth stalls, Facebook's continues. I can't say I am surprised. There, I find it possible to disagree without anyone threatening to kill me or my children. I find this reassuring. As I don't work in an office, I like the mundane chats, the silly jokes, the music. Sure, I will never get over the amount of cats and babies; though I have had both, I find them essentially boring. But I am not a fascist and accept this is something people do. Though I would no more photograph my cat than sext Philip Hammond.

Mostly I show off or moan. Both are pleasurable. But increasingly I find the moral superiority about quitting social media in favour of real life somewhat grating. What does this even mean? The idea of "really sharing" as opposed to larking about online? This is usually accompanied by a parental rant about kids living on their phones, their lives mediated and somehow unlived. It is as if my generation spent their childhoods climbing trees instead of being passively plonked on the sofa watching godawful telly presented by paedophiles.

Sure there is a level of performance to social media. The sucking in of cheeks and stomachs and the constant presentation of femininity as something that needs to be "liked" was not invented by Instagram. Instead of tutting, educate your children about consent over imagery and explain that Google is not a primary source.

Yet we have this stupid anxiety because we cannot admit that social media is not the binary opposite of real life. It is real life. This is why studies such as the latest one from

Denmark somehow just perpetuate this smugness. Half the participants were given access to Facebook, the other half went cold turkey for a week. Those who had a break felt "55% less stressed". Comparing ourselves with our peers causes unhappiness, you see. May I just add here that the Danes, though materially well off, have high rates of depression. The study showed those who quit Facebook felt less lonely and more connected to real people.

These sorts of studies strike me as self-satisfied. Sure, take a break. A social media detox. Drink your Nutribullet green gunge instead of photographing it. Help the old lady next door. Have some spiritual connection instead of joking with friends who aren't even "real" online. After all, you have free choice over these free apps. If you are "addicted" and can no longer function, work or have relationships, then there is a problem. But this addiction model is questionable. Are we addicted to televison, reading, music? Why is chatting so bad? Why is having so much access to so much information dangerous? I can sit with the same old friend and have the same old conversation, or I can play with new people who tell me new things. Both are real. Both can be brilliant.

If Twitter is stagnating, then it is partly to do with its failure to deal with abuse but also its infantilisation of users. Do I want to "heart" a picture of some drowning refugees? No I don't.

Facebook, meanwhile, is bombarding us with ads, but it is also giving us a little more control over which "friends" see what. The point is that none of this is compulsory. You may connect or not. You may show off or not. You may find love or not. You may or may not win the popularity contest. For this, I am afraid, is essentially life. So don't bore me with your self-imposed sabbaticals; I accept you are a better person than me, who fully connects in a deeper way than I can manage.

For I am quite happy on social media, waving not drowning. My friends there will come and rescue me if I need help. For we have only connected. (728 words)

Source:

https://www.theguardian.com/commentisfree/2015/nov/11/dont-think-youre-superior-to-me-because-youre-not-on-facebook

Document 4

TOUCHPAD
WYSIWYG!
FIRMWARE!
HOLOGRAM
C.PU. RAM. HDTV. E-I-E-I-O
I NEED AN UPDATE!
AGENT 99? IS THAT YOU?
HELLO? HELLO?
??
IT'S A CLASSIC CASE OF TECH FATIGUE...
WWW.CARTOONADAY.COM

SUJET CCP- e3a N° 1: Synthèse

(4 documents, synthèse 400 mots +/- 10 %)
voir consignes précises pages 28 et 53

Document 1

From Dutch hospital to Afghan clinic: new VR app aims to link 8.5m doctors

Imagine you're a doctor in Swindon and a patient with a chewing tobacco habit turns up with unusual tongue lesions. What if you could, at the press of a few buttons, locate and get instant advice from the Mumbai-based world expert on cancers related to chewing tobacco?

This is the vision for a new app which aims to transform the way in which 8.5 million doctors around the world share their knowledge and skills.

MDLinking – an expert directory, instant messaging service and video source – began trialling a beta version for iPhones in May this year and aims to launch its full Apple and Android versions before 2017.

The Dutch startup, which has €2.5m of seed funding, has several hundred testers in the Netherlands, 4,000 registered doctors so far and is in talks with organisations including Médecins Sans Frontières and the Aga Khan Development Network (AKDN) about using its free software.

"The original idea was that if doctors worldwide connect with each other and share knowledge, healthcare will improve on a global level" says Alec Behrens, co-founder of Booking.com and founding partner of MDLinking.

(...)Many doctors are already using instant messaging tools to discuss patient cases. A 2015 survey found more than 30% of doctors surveyed said they were sending patient-related information over services such as WhatsApp.

(...)As well as being a directory and secure instant messaging tool (it only accepts vetted medical professionals), the start-up is using virtual reality technology to record operations from multiple viewpoints, to form an interactive teaching tool – especially for countries where operating theatres are scarce.

(...)Dr Gijs van Acker, a surgeon at Medisch Centrum Haaglanden hospital in the Netherlands, first created teaching videos for his vascular surgery website a decade ago. "One of my residents was Hans Flu, and when he started MDLinking I said, 'You need something that's educational'. We wanted to make something more intuitive than 2D films," he says.

They came up with virtual reality combined with the view-selection interface, allowing users to flick to different sections of the operation. Traditional teaching methods can't compete, according to van Acker, who says that dead body tissue loses its colour, so isn't the same teaching experience, while students observing actual operations are often distracted by nerves.

He has recorded four 3D operations for MDLinking so far and – thanks to a partnership providing Samsung equipment – these are viewable via mobiles and virtual reality headsets.(407 words)

Adapted from *The Guardian,* September 18, 2016

Document 2

Meditation in virtual reality: it's like French philosophy meets the Matrix

(...)Welcome – if you have the headset or appropriate app – to Deepak Chopra's latest venture: virtual reality (VR) meditation.

The new age entrepreneur and self-help guru unveiled the simulation, titled "Finding your true self", this week at the headquarters of Wevr, a VR firm in Silicon Beach, Los

Angeles' tech hub.

Chopra, who narrates the simulation, hopes to sell the experience via booths at airports, hospitals and other locations, and via phones and laptops enabled with VR platforms.

"In 20 minutes you get a journey to enlightenment. The goal is to feel grounded and understand yourself a little better," he told the Guardian. The technology, he said, facilitated an understanding of consciousness which eluded even René Descartes, the 17th century French philosopher. "He was good for his time but didn't have VR to take it to the next level."

A bold claim for a nascent technology more associated with gaming and pornography than reflection and contemplation. But Chopra, 68, has not built a lucrative brand and sold millions of books such as *The Seven Spiritual Laws of Success* through timidity.

Meditation's benefits – improved focus, lower stress, inner peace – require investments of time, effort and discipline which frustrate many would-be practitioners. A vast market, Chopra hopes for a simulation which mixes "insights, contemplation and entertainment".

Meditation purists may wonder if that is cheating. Those who simply wonder if it works will be able to find out when the product launches, perhaps in a few weeks. "Soon, very soon," said Anthony Batt, Wevr's co-founder. The app will cost $10, he said.

For that, according to a three-minute trailer shown to the *Guardian* and others at the company's headquarters, you get trippy graphics, heavy on purple, with otherworldly sound effects laid over statements which, depending on perspective, are insightful, gnomic or nonsense.

There was no paradox between finding your true self via virtual reality because everyday reality is itself a simulation, said Chopra. An insect with 100 eyes, for instance, views the world differently than a human.

"For 30 years people have been coming to my lectures saying they don't get it. Well now they can."

Asked if the simulation tried to cross Descartes, who coined the maxim "I think, thefore I am," with the science fiction film The Matrix, Chopra beamed. "Absolutely!"

(...)Strapping on a headset or peering at a computer screen were not inimical to contemplation, said Chopra. "I've never been too attached to tradition. We're an evolving species. If you don't keep up with technology you're not in touch with the zeitgeist and you may as well pack it in." (435 words)

Adapted from *The Guardian*, 17 August 2016

Document 3

Virtual reality may look cool, but it will feel empty without community

It's a great time to be in the virtual-reality business. While Facebook, Microsoft, Samsung and Google are investing billions in hardware, we're experiencing a content gold rush.

But many people making VR content today seem to think the endgame is creating an experience that fully conveys a place – a trip to Mars or the Grand Canyon.

(...)Such experiences are impressive, but they will never truly feel real until they can be shared, because reality is about more than places. It's about people.

A story: I once met a young man in VR named Eric. I spotted him standing alone at the edge of a digitally generated cliff. "Admiring the view?" I asked, being goofy. He looked me over wordlessly. (...)

We were in AltspaceVR, a Second Life-like virtual world that is one of several social platforms available to early adopters of VR with Oculus Rifts or competing headsets HTC Vives and Samsung Gear VRs. As rendered clouds slid past, he told me about Oklahoma City, where he lives. He was 15.

(...)"I'm probably the first person in Oklahoma to get virtual reality," he told me, in a tone that conveyed both pride and great, inconsolable loneliness.

After I peeled off my headset, I was alone in my living room, but the conversation hung onto me for days. Talking to Eric, my body had reacted as though I was having a conversation with a lonely teen, all sympathetic nerves, because I was having a conversation with a lonely teen. I felt something, and I felt for him. AltspaceVR isn't a particularly convincing environment – the avatars are blocky, the scenes roughly sketched – but Eric's crushing adolescent awkwardness made virtual reality feel truly real.

(...) We're still a long way from virtual worlds that can interact with players with anything near the unpredictability and candor of another human being. Interacting with people is still more visceral than anything graphics, stories or gameplay can achieve alone. There's no sense in trying to work against this. Working with it, as a design strategy, by making space for real social interactions within virtual environments, is extraordinarily effective. Forget real-looking; let's try for real-feeling. Morningstar and Farmer wrote that "Cyberspace may indeed change humanity, but only if it begins with humanity as it really is." I'd argue the same for virtual reality.

I may never find Eric again, but I think of him every time I head into a VR world. His awkwardness charged the air: when I stood next to him, I felt aware of our closeness, despite the 1,300 miles separating our physical bodies. For the length of our conversation, the electric strangeness of human proximity made everything else irrelevant. I was immersed.(473)

! Adapted from *The Guardian* 23 August 2016

Document 4

The Virtues of Reality

SINCE the 1990s, we've seen two broad social changes that few observers would have expected to happen together.

First, youth culture has become less violent, less promiscuous and more responsible. American childhood is safer than ever before. Teenagers drink and smoke less than previous generations. The millennial generation has fewer sexual partners than its parents, and the teen birthrate has traced a two-decade decline. (...)Young people are half as likely to have been in a fight than a generation ago. Teen suicides, binge drinking, hard drug use — all are down.

But over the same period, adulthood has become less responsible, less obviously adult. For the first time in over a century, more 20-somethings live with their parents than in any other arrangement. (...) More and more prime-age workers are dropping out of the work force — men especially, and younger men more so than older men, though female work force participation has dipped as well.

(...) I want to advance a technology-driven hypothesis: This mix of youthful safety and adult immaturity may be a feature of life in a society increasingly shaped by the internet's virtual realities.

It is easy to see how online culture would make adolescent life less dangerous. Pornography to take the edge off teenage sexual appetite. Video games instead of fisticuffs or contact sports as an outlet for hormonal aggression. (Once it was feared that porn and violent media would encourage real-world aggression; instead they seem to be replacing it.) (...). Online hangouts instead of keggers(1) in the field. More texting and driving, but less driving — one of the most dangerous teen activities — overall.

The question is whether this substitution is habit-forming and soul-shaping, and whether it extends beyond dangerous teen behavior to include things essential to long-term human flourishing — marriage, work, family, all that old-fashioned "meatspace" stuff.

That's certainly the impression left whenever journalists try to figure out why young people aren't marrying, or dating, or in some cases even seeking sex.(...) The same impression is left by research on younger men dropping out of the work force: Their leisure time is being filled to a large extent by gaming, and happiness studies suggest that they are pretty content with the trade-off

.(...)The keenest critics of how the internet shapes culture, writers like Sherry Turkle, are often hopeful that with time and experience we will learn better management strategies, which keep the virtual in its place before too many real goods are lost.

Such strategies may work for individuals and families. But the trends in the marketplace — ever-more-customized pornography, virtual realities that feel more and more immersive, devices and apps customized for addictive behavior — seem likely to overwhelm most attempts to enjoy the virtual only within limits. (458 words)

(;) a kegger *: une beuverie (d'étudiants)*

Adapted from The New York Times, August 20, 2016

SUJET CCP- e3a N° 1: QCM

voir barème p.74

We need a social media with heart that gives us time to think

Will Hutton, The Guardian 7 february 2016

On average, we check our smartphones 200 times a day – for emails, alerts, tweets or text messages. That's before using any one of our phone's multiple applications. It is a degree of connectivity to one another, and the world beyond, that is unparalleled. And it's difficult to imagine life without it – to be so connected is to have access to instant knowledge, instant exchange, instant laughter and
5   anger.

The darker side is where this connectivity is taking understanding and the very structure of the way we think. It's not obvious that the good <u>outweighs</u> the bad. Instantaneity is the new god – instantaneity of presence, of communication and response. I know one highly paid CEO who will reply promptly to an email, although he must receive hundreds in any single hour.

10   On one level it is admirable – the access and responsiveness is extraordinary. But on another, it is worrying. What possible depth of thought can be associated with such fast replies? All there can be is the retelling of <u>stock</u> positions and relying on <u>gut reactions</u>. There can't be challenge, debate and argument because these are time-consuming; at the very least, it will distract you from answering the bombardment of emails arriving every few minutes.

15   Tim Berners-Lee, inventor of the world wide web in 1989, <u>went out of his way</u> recently, at the Sundance launch of the film *ForEveryone.net*, to deplore the negativity and <u>bullying</u> of much social media, with Twitter particularly in his sights. In a fast world without much thought, retweets in particular, he argued, have become a driver of anger. Apparently, we are 10 times likelier to retweet an item that makes us angry than one that makes us happy. Thus the character of much social media
20   – bullying, misogynist, negative.

Berners-Lee called for a reinvention of social media; he wanted platforms that were both open and configured better to express "constructive criticism and harmony". The internet should be a force for good. Martha Lane Fox, tireless campaigner for better use of the net, reinforced his cry: we need social media with heart.

25   In a fast world without much thought, retweets in particular have become a driver of anger

It's hard not to agree with both of them, but equally hard to imagine what such a constructive social media network with heart would look like. Above all, it would have to be much slower. In his bestselling book *Thinking, Fast and Slow*, Nobel prize-winner Daniel Kahneman argued that the human mind is configured according to two basic systems. As we emerged as thinking primates, we
30   had to rely on fast, instinctive, emotional reflex thinking, especially to handle danger; instincts were a way of staying alive. This he calls System 1 thinking. It may often make mistakes, be irrational and rely on the subconscious, but it allows for fast decision-making, vital for survival.

System 2 thinking is slower and more deliberative. You marshal evidence, you exercise judgment, you discuss with others and you try to arrive at conclusions that will hold up. It is time-consuming, intellectual and hard. It would obviously be better if more decisions were subject to System 2 treatment, but in the hurly-burly of life it is just not possible.

We fall back on System 1, with all its inherent cognitive biases, to get through the day. We are over-optimistic, over-emotional, too readily influenced by the way a recent event has framed our thinking, too anxious to avert risk rather than seize opportunity for no other reason than this is where fast, intuitive System 1 thinking takes us. We simply have to rely on the intuitive to manage all the impulses hitting us.

With a smartphone in your hand, System 1 thinking becomes the dominant mode of thought. Nobody can handle the volume of data in 2016 without relying on ifeelings to come up with instantaneous responses, often triggered by how you see others reacting. There is less scope for deliberation and discussion – the pressure is to make a snap judgment and move on. I love this film, this article is deplorable/fantastic or politician X is a welcome breath of fresh air/duplicitous bastard.

One of the reasons there is so much misogyny on the web is that criticising a woman's looks and style is the default mode for too many men. There is no logical link between disapproving of the opinions of a woman and of her appearance, but System 1 thinking does not care.

Tim Berners-Lee and Martha Lane Fox are right: the internet is the greatest device for opening up the world ever devised. It is democratising and enabling. But that assumes its users draw on it to aid System 2 thinking. Plainly, there are times when we use it to inform key decisions – to find out about an illness, to research a holiday, to track a scientific breakthrough. But in the main the web is for skating and browsing. We drift round YouTube or Facebook to be diverted by the idiosyncratic or unusual; it's compulsive because of its endless capacity to divert us into a System 1 world of trivia and intuition.

Maybe Berners-Lee's call will be heeded and someone will come up with a heart-based social media network, in which one of the basic protocols will be time to think, but it seems improbable and its success uncertain. For the moment, we are stuck with what we have – social and wider public conversations that are more emotional and more angry than we are in reality.(...)

(920 words)

I. COMPREHENSION

Choisissez la réponse qui vous paraît la plus adéquate en fonction du sens du texte.

1. From line 1 to line 5 (paragraph 1), it should be understood that:

(A) we can't keep up with the amount of data we receive daily

(B) we use our smartphones at least 200 times a day

(C) there are more smartphone apps now than before

(D) our smartphones mostly help connect us to other people's negative feelings

2. From line 6 to line 9 (paragraph 2), it should be understood that:

(A) connectivity may have a bad influence on the way our brain works

(B) connectivity puts bosses under pressure

(C) those who master instantaneity are like gods

(D)connectivity is more positive than negative on the whole

3. From line 10 to line 14 (paragraph 3), it should be understood that:

(A) instantaneity stimulates in-depth thinking

(B) the speed of internet exchanges triggers reflex rather than rational responses

(C) this kind of communication is only good for stock exchange transactions

(D) We don't like to spend time on challenges

4. From line 15 to line 20 (paragraph 4), it should be understood that:

(A) Tim Berners-Lee used to be in favour of bullying on social media

(B) social media makes people misogynistic

(C) the inventor of the internet is worried at the turn social media is taking

(D) There is a lot of violent criticism of social media

5. From line 21 to line 25 (paragraphs 5 &6) , it should be understood that:

(A) Twitter traduces widespread anger

(B)Twitter gives users motives to complain

(C) Internet-savvy people would like to see a different kind of internet

(D) anger triggered by tweets has become a major positive force on the net

6. From line 26 to line 32 (paragraph 7), it should be understood that:

(A) it is impossible to devise social media that will allow time for people to think

(B) we can't use our hearts on the net, only our brains

(C) aggressive response is natural to the way our brain works

(D) Humans are still too primitive to be able to ponder answers before they click

7. From line 33 to line 36 (paragraph 8), it should be understood that:

(A) we never use System 2 thinking in everyday life

(B) System 2 thinking tends to inhibit decisions and responses

(C) System 2 thinking is an activity which we enjoy

(D) the writer wishes people would use System 2 thinking more when interacting on social media

8. From line 37 to line 41 (paragraph 9), it should be understood that:

(A) System 1 thinking relies on imperfect knowledge

(B) the writer believes intuition is the best guide to our actions

(C) selecting System 1 or System 2 thinking is a deliberate choice we make

(D) we are never influenced by recent events when using System 2 thinking

9. From line 42 to line 47 (paragraph 10), it should be understood that:

(A) a smartphone makes us feel that we have to respond to anything we see

(B) our intuitions are more powerful than other people's responses

(C) System 2 thinking is adverse to ifeelings

(D) our smartphone responses are often simplistic and therefore inaccurate

10. From line 48 to line 50 (paragraph 11), it should be understood that:

(A) the way some women respond on social networks makes some men more misogynistic

(B) the way women look on social networks elicits mysogynistic comments

(C) System 1 thinking encourages misogynistic comments

(D) there is a link between what women say and the remarks they get

11. From line 51 to line 57 (paragraph 12), it should be understood that:

(A) the very reason why we surf the net is our preference for System 1 thinking

(B) the internet is getting more and more democratic

(C) we tend to look for familiar stuff on the internet

(D) people should use system 2 thinking to improve the internet

12. From line 58 to line 61 (paragraph 13), it should be understood that:

(A) social media makes us angrier and more emotional generally

(B) Berners-Lee's call is a voice clamouring in the desert

(C) the writer has doubts about the business future of a social media requiring time

(D) there is no way out of the bullying and misogyny on social media

II. LEXIQUE

Choisissez la réponse qui vous paraît la plus appropriée en fonction du contexte.

(les mots sont soulignés dans le texte)

13. outweighs (line 7) means :

(A)annuls

(B)outgrows

(C)offsets

(D)exceeds

14. stock (line 12) means :

(A)usual

(B)share

(C)commonplace

(D)simplistic

15. gut reactions (line 12) means :

(A) good reactions

(B)emotional responses

(C)nasty responses

(D)violent reactions

16. went out of his way (line 15) means :

(A)made an appearance

(B)changed his habits

(C)changed his usual line of discourse

(D) gave himself great pains

17. bullying (line 16) means :

(A)verbal intimidation

(B)brutal rites of initiation

(C)sexist harassment

(D)negative eloquence

18. marshal (line 33) means :

(A)avoid

(B)seek

(C)organize

(D)eliminate

18. hurly-burly (line 36) means :

(A)tumult

(B)race

(C)chaos

(D)contest

19. biases (line 37) means :

(A)mistakes

(B)roots

(C)distortions

(D)flaws

20. to come up with (line 43) means :

(A)find

(B)answer

(C)react

(D)imitate

21. snap (line 45) means :

(A)negative

(B)dismissive

(C)polite

(D)hasty

22. idiosyncratic (line 55) means :

(A)extremely silly

(B)very original

(C)solipsistic

(D)very bizarre

23. trivia (line 57) means :

(A)quizzes

(B)questions

(C)inessential facts

(D)impulsive answers

24. heeded (line 58) means :

(A) heard

(B)overlooked

(C)ignored

(D)echoed

III. COMPETENCE GRAMMATICALE

Choisissez la phrase correcte.

25.

(A) The people whose posts we respond to on social media

(B) The people which posts we respond to on social media

(C) The people the posts of which we respond to on social media

(D) the people whom posts we respond to on social media

26.

A) I am not used to going on Facebook

(B) I didn't use to going on Facebook

(C) I am not used to go on Facebook

(D)I havent used to go on Facebook

27.

(A) Instant messaging demand that she respond with the speed of lightning

(B) Instant messaging demands she respond with the speed of lightning

(C) Instant messaging demands that she responds with the speed of lightning

(D)Instant messaging demands that she respond with the speed of lightning

28.

(A) This 3D headset costed me a week's wages

(B) This 3D headset cost me a week wages

(C) This 3D headset cost me a week's wages

(D)This 3D headset costs me a week wages

29.

(A) Social media with heart is the lesser of two evils

(B) Social media with heart is the less of two evils

(C) Social media with heart is the lower of two evils

(D)Social media with heart is the fewer of two evils

30.

(A) Pokémon Go went off last July

(B) (D)Pokémon Go came out last July

(C) Pokémon Go went out last July

(D)Pokémon Go came off last July

31.

(A) No sooner had it come out but millions of 'trainers' started roaming the streets

(B) No sooner it came out than millions of 'trainers' started roaming the streets

(C) No sooner had it come out as millions of 'trainers' started roaming the streets

(D) No sooner did it come out than millions of 'trainers' started roaming the streets

32.If you want to tweet, you … better get ready for some bullying

(A) should

(B) must

(C) had

(D)might

33.Not everybody on Facebook gets ... posts and pictures shared

(A) his

(B) her

(C) their

(D) your

34.Martha Lane Fox is ... Tim Berners-Lee on the necessity to make internet more humane

(A) of the same mind as

(B) the same mind as

(C) at the same opinion as

(D) at the same mind as

35.The Facebook interface is more flexible and interactive than ... Twitter

(A) on

(B) that one of

(C) that of

(D)the one of

36.Connecting or not connecting is...

(A) any users' choice

(B) any user's choice

(C) the choice of any user's

(D)any user choice

37. in terms of social network innnovation, no one knows what the future may

(A) hold

(B) have

(C) be holding

(D) be having

38.The … users, the … the fun

(A) less... greater

(B) more... greater

(C) less... fewer

(D)more... less

39. … Google … launched

(A) It's 18 years ago that... has been

(B) It's been 18 years since... has been

(C) It's been 18 years since...was

(D) It's for 18 years that … was

CCP- e3a Sujet n°2 A : Synthèse

Document 1

How water shortages flow into collaboration not war

(...)Water matters. Across the world, we are running out of the stuff. Not absolutely, but where we want it and when we want it. Everyone expects "water wars": Amazon offers seven books with that title. But what if the real story is how water shortages promote the politics of cooperation rather than conflict? (...)

The Water Kingdom tells what British science writer Philip Ball calls the "secret history" of China. From its founding, Chinese society has been organised around the management of water. Dynasties rose and fell according to whether they could control the floods that came down the Yellow River along with the rich, fertile silt in which its citizens planted their crops.

(...)Through all the twists and turns in the long and uninterrupted history of Chinese civilisation, the control of water has been the single unifying thread. And Ball's vibrant narrative makes magnificent sense of it all, from Yu to Chairman Mao, whose Communist control included building more dams than any leader in history, and his successors. Confronted by droughts that have dried up the Yellow River, today's leaders of the Water Kingdom have responded by building giant canals to bring replenishing waters from the Yangtze in the wet south.

Controlling the great rivers of China has always required an iron imposition of central power. And when war intervened, things went badly wrong. In 1938, to block advancing Japanese invaders, Chinese generals broke the Yellow River's dykes. Result: hundreds of thousands of deaths, almost all of them Chinese peasants caught up in floods and famine as the river swept south across its heavily populated floodplain.

China was and remains the ultimate hydraulic civilisation. As Ball puts it: "China's water will decide its future." And in many ways the American West in the 20th century proved a worthy successor. By harnessing the mighty River Colorado, which runs south from Colorado to Mexico, and distributing its waters to farmers and cities, modern engineers have sustained shining civilisations around desert cities such as Los Angeles, Phoenix and Las Vegas.

Tensions were never far away as city bosses, state governors and agribusiness corporations jostled for the Colorado's waters – tensions immortalised in the 1974 movie *Chinatown*. But Fleck's engaging journalistic odyssey, *Water is For Fighting Over*, like Ball's, finds that fighting has been noticeably absent. Instead, the need to harness water in an arid land meant deals were ultimately done, power was brokered, sluices stayed open, and the water kept flowing.

Fleck showcases the networks of little-known technocrats who have done the deals, and slowly encouraged their masters to adopt limits on once-profligate water use. Even in Las Vegas. Behind the showy glitz of its ostentatious hotel fountains, Vegas today is a model of water conservation, he says. Since 2000, its population has grown 34 per cent while its water use has fallen by 26 per cent.

Fleck argues persuasively that the battle for water is not a zero-sum game. Savings can be made. Deals today may involve a city in one state investing in water conservation on farms in another state, so as to lay claim to the "saved" water. Today Californians irrigate golf courses rather than alfalfa. Ultimately, "when people have less water, they use less water", he says.

He makes his case well. But that doesn't mean the conflicts aren't real. Nor that there aren't losers as well as winners. The losers, as every last drop of Colorado water has been divided up in the US, have been nature and Mexicans. (582 words)

adapted from The New Scientist, 31 August 2016

Document 2

California's Drought Is Part of a Much Bigger Water Crisis

) every state west of the Rockies has been facing a water shortage of one kind or another in recent years. California's is a severe, but relatively short-term, drought. But the Colorado River basin — which provides critical water supplies for seven states including California — is the victim of a slower-burning catastrophe entering its 16th year. Wyoming, Colorado, New Mexico, Utah, Nevada, Arizona and California all share water from the Colorado River, a hugely important water resource that sustains 40 million people in those states, supports 15 percent of the nation's food supply, and fills two of the largest water reserves in the country.

The severe shortages of rain and snowfall have hurt California's $46 billion agricultural industry and helped raise national awareness of the longer-term shortages that are affecting the entire Colorado River basin. But while the two problems have commonalities and have some effect on one another, they're not exactly the same thing.

Most of California is experiencing "extreme to exceptional drought," and the crisis has now entered its fourth year. This month, signaling how serious the current situation is, state officials announced the first cutback to farmers' water rights since 1977, and ordered cities and towns to cut water use by as much as 36 percent.

(...)A half-decade of torrential rains might bail California out of its crisis, but the larger West's problems are more structural and systemic. "Killing the Colorado"(1) has shown that people are entitled to more water from the Colorado than has flowed through it, on average, over the last 110 years. Meanwhile much of the water is lost, overused or wasted, stressing both the Colorado system, and trickling down to California, which depends on the Colorado for a big chunk of its own supply. Explosive urban growth matched with the steady planting of water-thirsty crops – which use the majority of the water – don't help. Arcane laws actually encourage farmers to take even more water from the Colorado River and from California's rivers than they actually need, and federal subsidies encourage farmers to plant some of the crops that use the most water.

(...)While there are mixed views on whether climate change can be blamed for

California's drought, a recent National Oceanic and Atmospheric Administration (NOAA) report found climate change was not the cause. Global warming has caused excessive heat that may have worsened the drought's effects, but it isn't necessarily to blame for the lack of rain. It's true that recent years have yielded much less rain and snow than previous times in history, the NOAA report explains, but that's just a result of "natural variance" and not necessarily because of man-made pollution. But in both California and the larger Colorado River basin, mismanagement of the water supply has left the West more vulnerable to both short and long-term changes in climate.

When officials divvied up rights to Colorado River water nearly a century ago, it happened to be a wetter period than usual. The result? The states vastly overestimated the river's annual flow. Today, the river's reserves are especially low and states are still claiming the same amount of water from the Colorado River that they always have — which is 1.4 trillion gallons a year more than the river actually produces.(540 words)

Adapted from *ProPublica*, June 25, 2015

(1)A documentary.

Document 3

Millions exposed to dangerous lead levels in US drinking water, report finds

More than 18 million Americans are served drinking water by providers that have violated federal laws concerning lead in water, with only a tiny proportion of offenses resulting in any penalty, a new report has found.

The toxic water crisis in Flint, Michigan, is "not anomalous", the Natural Resources Defense Council (NRDC) report states, with widespread violations of national rules designed to protect people from lead, a known neurotoxin that is harmful even in small doses.

NRDC's analysis of US Environmental Protection Agency (EPA) data shows that 5,363 water systems, which provide water to more than 18 million people, breached the federal

Lead and Copper Rule last year. These violations include the failure to properly test water for lead or inadequate treatment of water to prevent lead from leeching from old pipes into the drinking supply.

The violations occurred across virtually every US state last year. Most seriously, 1,110 community water utilities provided water that exceeded the EPA's actionable limit for lead in water. This means that more than 3.9 million Americans were exposed to dangerously high levels of lead in 2015.

Despite the widespread failure of water suppliers across the US, very few were punished by the EPA last year. Of more than 8,000 violations of federal laws, enforcement action was only taken against 11% of cases. Penalties were sought for just 3% of violations, meaning there is "no cop on the beat", according to the NRDC.

In a statement, the EPA said it recognized there are "ongoing challenges in compliance with the Lead and Copper Rule".

"The agency has intensified work with state drinking water programs with a priority focus on implementation of the rule, including engagement with every state drinking water program across the country to ensure they are addressing any high lead levels and fully implementing the current rule," the regulator said.

The EPA said that many water systems that violated the rules in 2015 have already resolved their problems. A revised Lead and Copper rule won't appear until 2017 at the earliest, despite the widespread problems in Flint and beyond.

"Flint symbolizes how disastrous the gaps are in the system and there really is a much broader problem across America," said Erik Olson, director of NRDC's health program. "Americans take for granted that the water flowing from their taps is clean and safe but that assumption is often false.

"Providing safe drinking water to citizens is a fundamental government service. If you're not doing that, you're not doing your job. Unsafe drinking water is a national problem and it needs a national solution."

Olson said that water utilities are routinely "gaming the system" to underplay the amount of lead found in water. The Guardian has revealed that at least 33 US cities have used various methods that can mask the true level of lead when conducting tests.

(...)Flint's water is now considered by the EPA to be safe to drink if a filter is used. However, some lawmakers have voiced concerns that more needs to be done to avoid a repeat of the disaster that befell the Michigan city.

"Flint wasn't an isolated example," said Dick Durbin, a Democrat senator. "We need a coordinated effort at all levels, we need people in communities to speak up so they don't become the next Flint."(552 words)

Adapted from *The Guardian*, June 28, 2016

Document 4

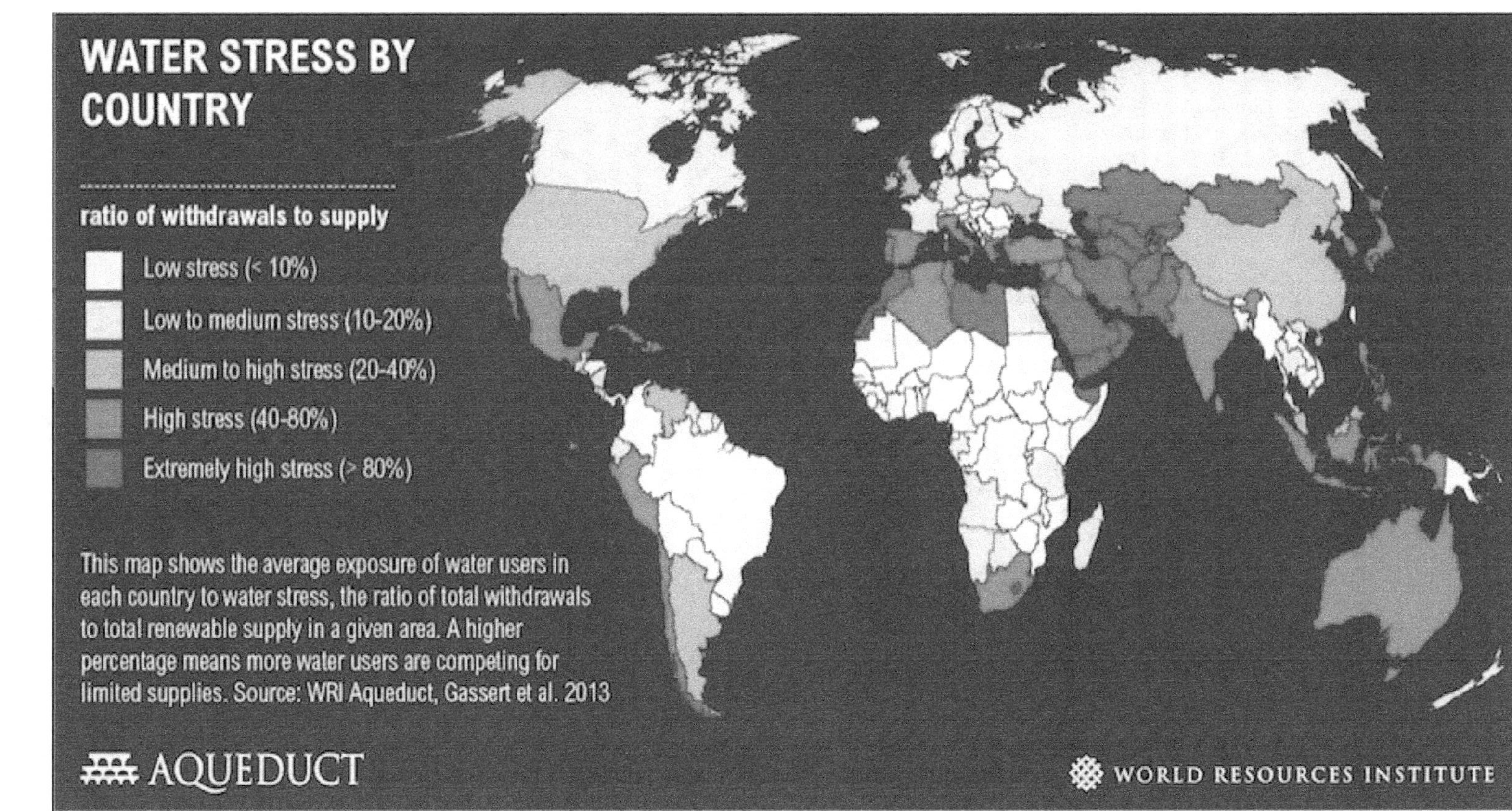

WATER STRESS BY COUNTRY
ratio of withdrawals to supply
Low stress (< 10%)
Low to medium stress (10-20%)
Medium to high stress (20-40%)
High stress (40-80%)
Extremely high stress (> 80%)
This map shows the average exposure of water users in each country to water stress, the ratio of total withdrawals to total renewable supply in a given area. A higher percentage means more water users are competing for limited supplies. Source: WRI Aqueduct, Gassert et al. 2013
AQUEDUCT
WORLD RESOURCES INSTITUTE

CCP- e3a - Sujet n°2 B: QCM

Sujet d'entraînement CCP-e3a n° 2 – B : QCM

Police Violence: American Epidemic, American Consent

Charles M. Blow *The New York Times,* SEPT. 26, 2016

Another set of black men killed by the police — one in Tulsa, Okla., another in Charlotte, N.C.

Another set of protests, and even some rioting.

Another television cycle in which the pornography of black death, pain and anguish are exploited for visual sensation and ratings gold.

5   And yes, another moment of mistakenly focusing on individual cases and individual motives and individual protests instead of recognizing that what we are witnessing in a wave of actions rippling across the country is an exhaling — a primal scream, I would venture — of cumulative cultural injury and a frantic attempt to <u>stanch</u> the bleeding from multiplying wounds.

We can no longer afford to buy into the delusion that this moment of <u>turmoil</u> is about <u>discrete</u> cases
10   or their specific disposition under the law. The system of justice itself is under interrogation. The cultural mechanisms that produced that system are under interrogation. America as a whole is under interrogation.

We are in a new age in which the <u>shroud</u> has slipped and trauma has risen.

This is a video age, in which facts that were previously filtered though police accounts and media
15   sources, that were previously whispered over shoulders at barbershops and across kitchen tables, have been <u>buttressed </u>by the immediacy and veracity of visual proof.

It is an age in which the language of resistance has been set and accepted, in which the mode of expression and resistance has been demonstrated and proved effective. It is an age of enlightenment and anger, of fear and frustration, of activism and alertness. Black America is beyond the breaking
20   point, a point of no return.

And in this <u>era</u>, the discussion around these issues must be broad and deep because the actions required to address the problems must be broad and deep.

This moment in our nation's history is not about how individual fears are articulated — in an emergency call, in an officer's response, in weapons drawn and fired, in black people's desire to
25 flee for their lives, in black parents' anxiety about the safety of their children. This moment is about the enormous, almost invisible structure that informs those fears — the way media and cultural presentations disproportionately display black people, and black men in particular, as dangerous and menacing and criminal. It's about the way historical policies created our modern American ghettos and their concentrated poverty; the ways in which such concentrated poverty and its blight and

30 hopelessness can be a prime breeding ground for criminal behavior; the way these areas make poverty sticky and opportunity scarce; the way resources, from education to health care to nutrition, are limited in these areas.

We keep talking about choices, but we don't talk nearly enough about the fact that choices are always made within a cultural and historical context.

35 People didn't simply choose to live in neighborhoods with poor housing and poor schools and crumbling infrastructure and few grocery stores and fewer adequate health care facilities. There were many factors that created those neighborhoods: white flight, and the black flight of wealthier black people, community disinvestment, business lending practices and government policies assigning infrastructure and public transportation to certain parts of cities and not others.

40 And the people living in those communities — sometimes trapped in those communities — make choices, sometimes poor ones, within that context.

We may say that a poor choice is simply wrong and the offending party must deal with the consequences. But poor choices made in a poor environment don't have the same consequences as those made in wealthy environments. For poor people, the same poor choices are punished more
45 often and more severely, compounding their deficit.

Then America takes it further, imputing the poor choices of a few onto a whole race, and in so doing sets the stage for disaster. This creates the suspicion and fear that can lead to the deaths we're seeing, in which the person killed may have made no poor choices, in which the only poor choice was the pulling of a trigger.

50 This is what people mean when they talk about the impact of systemic racism in these cases and in these areas. It is not that the police harbor more racism than the rest of America, but rather that racism across society, including within our police departments and system of justice, has been erected in ways that disproportionately impact poor, minority communities. That is acutely clear in these killings.

55 What took centuries to grow may take a long time to fully chop down. You can't fight racism by plucking leaves from the top of the poisonous tree, but by taking an ax to the root.

Republican vice-presidential candidate Mike Pence said last week, "We ought to set aside this talk, this talk about institutional racism and institutional bias," calling it "rhetoric of division." That is exactly the opposite of what we should do.

60 The police are simply instruments of the state, and the state is the people who comprise it. The police are articulating a campaign of control and containment of populations and that campaign has the implicit approval of every citizen within their jurisdictions. This is not a rogue officer problem; this is a rogue society problem.

I. COMPREHENSION

Choisissez la réponse qui vous paraît la plus adéquate en fonction du sens du texte.

1. From line 1 to line 4, it should be understood that:

(A)US media always show the same boring things

(B)Showing such violence against black people on TV is like broadcasting X-rated films

(C)us the writer is fed up with riots and protests

(D)TV channels boost their ratings with series on black crime

2. From line 5 to line 8, it should be understood that:

(A)the writer is inviting his readers to focus on the facts of the cases in Tulsa and Charlotte

(B)the riots and protests are a response to an epidemic of police shootings

(C)there is a wave a violence from the police that traduces primitive impulses

(D)the police are desperate to control multiplying acts of black violence across the country

3. From line 9 to line 12, it should be understood that:

(A)the police are investigating the whole background behind those two cases

(B)the culture of collective violence in black people is being researched

(C)protesters are angry at the whole system rather than at individual deaths

(D)It is time for all Americans to become aware that protests are a serious issue

4. From line 13 to line 16, it should be understood that:

(A)rumours and hearsay are now contradicted by videos

(B)Some people are out of control and cause trauma to the nation

(C)reliable facts used to be available only through the police and the media

(D)Videos now offer evidence of what people used to know by word of mouth only

5. From line 17 to line 20, it should be understood that:

(A)It is no longer possible to stop Black America from defending itself

(B)enlightened, alert people in the Us are pitted against angry, frustrated people

(C) the writer disapproves the rise of self-defensive black activism

(D)many people in America still reject the language of black resistance

6. From line 21 to line 26 it should be understood that:

(A)it is time for individuals to learn to control their fears

(B)police overreaction is often due to fear

(C)the public should focus on general root causes rather than individual motives

(D)explanations about the origins of the violent acts do not matter

7. From line 26 to line 32, it should be understood that:

(A)the backdrop of indiscriminate police shootings of blacks is structural inequality

(B)most white people believe everything the media say about black crime

(C)black crime cannot be put down only to circumstances in which some black people live

(D)policies to contain black people in ghettos were deliberate

8. From line 33 to line 41, it should be understood that:

(A)black people who choose to live in deprived areas take risks

(B)the question of choice has been displaced by the media rhetoric

(C)the poorer black residents tend to be hostile to whites and wealthy blacks

(D) Context can't explain everything

9. From line 42 to line 45, it should be understood that:

(A)the law should not sanction people from deprived neighborhoods as harshly as others

(B)punishment by law adds to the woes of people living in crime-ridden areas

(C)they can never improve their lot although they are given the same chances

(D) the criminal justice system and law enforcement are unfair to all citizens

10. From line 46 to line 49, it should be understood that:

(A)Black people are disproportionately punished when they use a firearm

(B)America causes black crime to rise by its cultural and institutional choices

(C) blacks are suspected of crime by association and punished even when innocent

(D)when policement shoot, even without cause, they are never punished

11. From line 50 to line 54, it should be understood that:

(A)unjustified killings are produced by a whole system, not just individual officers

(B)the police are responsible for systemic racism but are not more racist than the rest

(C)the latests killings are the outcome of increasing racism in law enforcement

(D)people who talk about systemic racism really target the police

12. From line 55 to line 63, it should be understood that:

(A)Mike Pence thinks blaming the system increases the likelihood of shootings

(B)the system is acting against the citizens' will and interests

(C)America as a whole is responsible for the unjustified shooting deaths of innocents

(D)the writer disapproves of people who criticize the criminal justice system

II. LEXIQUE

Choisissez la réponse qui vous paraît la plus appropriée en fonction du contexte.

(les mots sont soulignés dans le texte)

13. stanch (line 8) means

(A)cause

(B)show

(C)stop

(D)wipe off

14. turmoil (line 9) means

(A)unrest

(B)anger

(C)panic

(D)anxiety

15. discrete (line 8) means

(A)unimportant

(B)individual

(C)disconnected

(D)personal

16. shroud (line 13) means

(A) moment

(B) opportunity

(C) veil

(D) lie

17. buttressed(line 16) means

A) disproved

(B) contradicted

(C) publicized

(D) reinforced

18. era (line 21) means

(A) time

(B) space

(C) sphere

(D) domain

18. flee (line 25) means

(A) fight

(B) run

(C) hit

(D) call

19. blight (line 29) means

(A) violence

(B) sadness

(C) ugliness

(D) curse

20. sticky (line 31) means

(A) tacky

(B) unbearable

(C) enduring

(D) worse

21. flight (line 37) means

(A) departure

(B) conflict

(C) hostility

(D) invasion

22. poor (line 41) means

(A) low

(B) needy

(C) ill-advised

(D) mediocre

23. compounding (line 45) means

(A) adding to

(B) improving

(C) fusing

(D) finishing off

24. harbour (line 51) means

(A) support

(B) hide

(C) promote

(D) exhibit

III. COMPETENCE GRAMMATICALE

Choisissez la phrase correcte.

25.

(A) Black are twice as likely as white to be pulled over by the road police

(B) Blacks are twice likely as whites to be pulled off by the road police

(C) Blacks are twice as likely as whites to be pulled over by the road police

(D) Blacks are twice as likely as whites to be pulled off by the road police

26.

(A) To this day official homicide rates by the police in the US have never been disclosed

(B) To this day official rates of homicides by the police in the US were never disclosed

(C) To this day official homicides by the police rates in the US have never been disclosed

(D) To this day official homicide by the police rates in the US were never disclosed

27.

(A) The Obama administration record in terms of racial equality is poor

(B) The Obama's administation record in terms of racial equality is poor

(C) The Obama administration's record in terms of racial equality is poor

(D) Obama administration's record in terms of racial equality is poor

28.

(A) Equal justice is one of America defining issues

(B) Equal justice is a defining issue of America

(C) Equal justice is one of America's defining issue

(D) Equal justice is a defining issue of America's

29.

(A) The incarceration rate of black is 6 times the one of white

(B) The incarceration rate of blacks is 6 times that of whites

(C) The incarceration rate of blacks is 6 times the one of whites

(D)The incarceration rate of blacks is 6 times the same as whites

30.

(A) The US is one of the few truly multicultural country of the world

(B) The US are one of the few truly multicultural countries of the world

(C) The US is one of the few truly multicultural countries of the world

(D) The US are ones of the few truly multicultural countries of the world

31.

(A) civil rights have been the centerpiece of the Democrats' agenda since the 1960s

(B) civil rights are the centerpiece of the Democrats agenda since the 1960s

(C) civil rights were the centerpiece of the Democrats agenda from the 1960s

(D) civil rights have been the centerpiece of the Democrat agenda since the 1960s

32.

(A) Everybody cannot live in crime-free, affluent neighborhoods

(B) Not everybody can live in crime-free, affluent neighborhoods

(C) Anybody cannot live in crime-free, affluent neighborhoods

(D) Nobody cannot live in crime-free, affluent neighborhoods

33. This is the magistrate ... they appointed as prosecutor in the case

(A) which

(B) who

(C) whom

(D) whose

34. They are investigating the scene of the shooting, and all the circumstances...

(A) thereof

(B) of them

(C) of which

(D) of the one

35. In many cases, unfortunately, circumstances are... clear

(A) not the most

(B) completely not

(C) nothing but

(D) all but

36.unsatisfactory …, the grand jury's decision is final

(A) it can be

(B) as much as it can be

(C) as it would be

(D) though it may be

37.Civil rights groups... some community building in order to prevent those shootings

(A) have been attempting

(B) has been attempting

(C) are being attempting

(D) were attempted

38.The whole report on the investigation... in ... of the New York Times

(A) has been published... yesterday's edition ...

(B) was published... the yesterday edition ...

(C) was published... yesterday's edition ...

(D) has been published... the yesterday edition...

39.They will disclose the circumstances as soon as...

(A) those are known

(B) those will be known

(C) those are being known

(D) those know

CCP- e3a Sujet n°3 A : Synthèse

Document 1

What is the U.S. Commitment in Paris?

The United States has joined 185 countries in promising to curb carbon dioxide and other greenhouse gas emissions, develop other ways to mitigate the impacts and to make communities more resilient to climate change.

(...)So what exactly is the United States proposing to do?

The United States has committed to reduce its greenhouse gas emissions by 26-28 percent below the 2005 level in 2025, and to make "best efforts" to reduce emissions by 28 percent. That would include curbs on carbon dioxide, methane, nitrous oxide, perfluorocarbons, sulfur hexafluoride and nitrogen trifluoride, all of which contribute to global warming.

How will we do that? The United States already is taking measures that will help reduce emissions. The nation can continue that effort by becoming more efficient in how we use energy in everything from buildings and cars to washing machines and cell phones; using a greater portion of alternative energies like solar and wind over fossil fuels; and developing better technologies for energy storage, and for the capture, storage and recycling of carbon.

All of that could take place through a combination of laws, regulations and incentives— Congress and the courts willing. That includes regulations under the Clean Air Act that would force electric power plants to reduce their carbon emissions; and grants and tax incentives to propel the development of more alternative energy sources like wind and solar power.

The power sector now accounts for 31 percent of U.S. emissions. Efforts to upgrade the electricity grid to better accommodate intermittent sources like solar and wind would help, as would development of better energy storage technologies.

The efforts to date have put the U.S. on a path to reduce emissions 17 percent below the 2005 level by 2020. To reach the new 2025 goal, the nation will have to double the pace.

Here's a look at key ways we're cutting emissions:

Fuel economy standards: Transportation accounts for about 27 percent of U.S. emissions. The government has been setting "corporate average fuel economy" standards since 1975 —requiring automakers to meet an average miles-per-gallon standard for their products (with exceptions), or pay a penalty.

(...)Buildings and appliances: The Department of Energy is preparing measures to curb emissions by setting energy conservation standards for appliances and other types of equipment, and building code standards for commercial and residential buildings. Many of these standards already exist; they are likely to become stronger.

Power plants: 31 percent of greenhouse gas emissions come from the production of electricity, most of which relies on fossil fuels, mostly natural gas and coal. The Clean Power Plan established by the EPA under the Clean Air Act sets goals for each state to cut carbon pollution, and allows states to come up with their own plans to meet those goals. The plan is likely to greatly reduce reliance on coal, which is the most polluting fuel. The plan has been challenged in Congress and the courts.

(...)Financial and aid commitments: (...)This week, Secretary of State John Kerry told the climate gathering that the United States also will double its commitment to $861 million in grant-based investments to help developing nations find ways to adapt to climate change. To what extent the U.S. Congress will go along with that remains to be seen.(...)
(546 words)

Adapted from *The Earth Institute (1)* – December 11, 2015

(1)A department of the University of Columbia.

Document 2

China's coal peak hailed as turning point in climate change battle

The global battle against climate change has passed a historic turning point with China's huge coal burning finally having peaked, according to senior economists.

They say the moment may well be a significant milestone in the course of the Anthropocene, the current era in which human activity dominates the world's environment.

China is the world's biggest polluter and more than tripled its coal burning from 2000 to 2013, emitting billions of tonnes of climate-warming carbon dioxide. But its coal consumption peaked in 2014, much earlier than expected, and then began falling.

The economists argue in a new paper on Monday that this can now be seen as permanent trend, not a blip, due to major shifts in the Chinese economy and a crackdown on pollution.

"I think it is a real turning point," said Lord Nicholas Stern, an eminent climate economist at the London School of Economics, who wrote the analysis with colleagues from Tsinghua University in Beijing. "I think historians really will see [the coal peak of] 2014 as a very important event in the history of the climate and economy of the world."

(...)The struggle to tame climate change and avoid the "severe, widespread, and irreversible" damage predicted by scientists is often seen as too difficult. Even the successful global climate deal signed in Paris in December is not yet enough to hold world temperatures below a 2C rise, which is seen as the danger limit, and will need to be ratcheted up.

But Stern said he thought the breakthrough in China would drive further action by other nations: "Given the international political and economic structures we now have to manage climate change, I think it will be very influential on others."

(...)To enter into force, the Paris climate deal requires the majority of large emitting nations to ratify it. Espinosa said: "I hope these positive developments reported today will encourage more countries to step forward so that Paris enters into force sooner rather than later."

Stern said that China's progress indicates its total carbon emissions will start falling before 2025, well ahead of its official target date of 2030 (...) The peaking of China's coal use is very significant, Schellnhuber said: "It is a turning point and very good news." But he argues that another, steeper, downturn in coal burning will be needed in future to stabilise the global climate.

"If we take the 2C target seriously, coal really has to disappear," he said. "I think coal will have to be phased out completely in all countries of the world by about 2035." Schellnhuber, one of the world's most influential climate scientists, said in 2015 that an "induced implosion" of the fossil fuel industry was required to beat climate change.

(...)Stern said there are a series of deep and long-term transformations taking place in China, which means the nation's falling coal use is now a permanent trend. One is the falling rate of economic growth from 9-10% to about 6% and the transformation of the Chinese economy away from heavy industry and towards more hi-tech and service sectors, which are much less dependent on energy.

There is also a serious focus on improving energy efficiency, he said, to avoid dependency on imported fuels.

Another critical factor is a major policy shift from the Chinese government to tackle the pollution of air and water that blights many citizens. Stern said China's emergence as a global power in recent decades was important too, as well as its self-interest in avoiding global warming.

"It is partly the sense of responsibility that China really does feel" as a global power, he said. "But it is also climate change itself. Water has dominated Chinese thinking for millennia and its major rivers come off the Himalayas. What happens to the Himalayas and its ice caps is absolutely crucial to China, and of course climate change is mostly a water phenomenon."(...) (650 words)

Adapted from *The Guardian,* 25 July 2016

Document 3

China and US ratify COP21 Paris climate agreement

The United States and China on Saturday formally joined the Paris climate change agreement, with President Barack Obama hailing the accord as the "moment we finally decided to save our planet".

The move by the world's two biggest polluters is a major step forward for the 180-nation deal, which sets ambitious goals for capping global warming and funnelling trillions of dollars to poor countries facing climate catastrophe.

Obama and his Chinese counterpart Xi Jinping handed ratification documents to UN chief Ban Ki-moon, who said he was now optimistic the agreement will be in force by the end of this year.

(...)The US and China are together responsible for some 40 percent of the world's emissions, so their participation is crucial.

(...)Until Saturday only 24 of the signatories had ratified the accord, including France and many island states threatened by rising sea levels but who only produce a tiny proportion of the world's emissions.

(...) 'Powerful signal'

Climate is one of the few areas where the world's two most powerful countries -- who are at loggerheads on issues ranging from trade disputes, cyberspying and the South China Sea -- are able to find common cause.

Campaigners welcomed the move, with WWF saying they had sent "a very powerful signal that there will be real global action on climate change".

But some environmental groups say that the Paris pledges by China, the US and others fall far short of what is needed to meet the goal of less than two degrees of warming.

"This moment should be seen as a starting point, not the finale, of global action on climate," said Greenpeace policy adviser Li Shuo.

The Paris pact calls for capping global warming at well below two degrees Celsius (3.6 degrees Fahrenheit), and 1.5 C (2.7 F) if possible, compared with pre-industrial levels.

For China, ratifying the agreement fits with Beijing's domestic political agenda of being seen to make efforts to clean up the environment, after years of breakneck industrial development led to soaring air, water and ground pollution.

The scourge is estimated to have caused hundreds of thousands of early deaths, and is the source of mounting public anger.

Under the Paris accord, China has pledged to cut its carbon emissions per unit of GDP by 60-65 percent from 2005 levels by 2030 and increase non-fossil fuel sources in primary energy consumption to about 20 percent.

Neither of those requirements implies a commitment to cut absolute levels of emissions, although China is also obliged to have them peak by "around 2030".

In its Paris commitment, the US promised to cut its own emissions 26-28 percent below 2005 levels by 2025.

During the negotiations over the Paris deal Beijing stressed the concept of "differentiated responsibilities" -- the idea that developed countries should shoulder the lion's share of the burden as they have polluted most since the Industrial Revolution.

For its part the White House is looking for the Paris accord to come into force during Obama's tenure, in part to burnish his climate legacy, but also to ensure it is not derailed by the forthcoming US election.

The administration has been careful to structure the agreement so that it can be enacted by Obama under existing presidential authorities and without Congressional approval.(...)
(552 words)

Adapted from AFP – NEWS Wires - September 3, 2016

Brexit Armageddon was a terrifying vision – but it simply hasn't happened

Larry Elliott, *The Guardian,* 20 August 2016

Unemployment would rocket. Tumbleweed would billow through deserted high streets. Share prices would crash. The government would struggle to find buyers for UK bonds. Financial markets would be in meltdown. Britain would be plunged instantly into another deep recession.

Remember all that? It was hard to avoid the <u>doom and gloom</u>, not just in the weeks leading up to
5 the referendum, but in those immediately after it. Many of those who voted remain comforted themselves with the certain knowledge that those who had voted for Brexit would suffer a bad case of buyer's remorse.

It hasn't worked out that way. The 1.4% jump in retail sales in July showed that consumers have not stopped spending, and seem to be more influenced by the weather than they are by fear of the
10 consequences of what happened on 23 June.

(...)The financial markets are serene. Share prices are close to a record high, and fears that companies would find it difficult and expensive to borrow have proved wide of the mark. Far from <u>dumping</u> UK government gilts, pension funds and insurance companies have been keen to hold on to them.

15 City economists had predicted an immediate rise in the claimant count measure of unemployment in July. That hasn't happened either. This week's figures show that instead of a 9,000 rise, there was an 8,600 drop.

<u>Some caveats are in order</u>. It is still early days. Hard data is <u>scant</u>. Survey evidence is still consistent with a slowdown in the economy in the second half of 2016. Brexit may be a slow burn, with the
20 impact only becoming apparent in the months and years to come.

But it is obvious that the sky has not fallen in as a result of the referendum, and those who said it would look a bit silly. By now, Britain was supposed to be <u>reeling from</u> the emergency budget George Osborne said would be necessary to fill a £30bn black hole in the public finances caused by a plunging economy. The emergency budget is history, as is Osborne.
25 In a way, Project Fear did work. <u>It put the wind up</u> businesses, making them <u>warier</u> about investing in new kit. And at least some of the people who voted remain did so because they were worried about the economic consequences of leaving. That was hardly surprising, given the regular and lurid warnings – from the Treasury, the Bank of England, the International Monetary Fund and the Organisation for Economic Cooperation and Development – about the dire consequences that would
30 inevitably flow from Brexit.

The British state did an abrupt U-turn on 24 June. Having failed to secure a yes vote, the official position had to change fast. The imperative was to get all those people who had been frightened witless <u>to chill out</u>. Some surveys since the Brexit vote did indeed pick up an abrupt drop in consumer confidence. The government feared a recession of its own making.

35 So instead of telling the public how hard life was going to be outside the EU, ministers and officials sought to reassure, to administer large doses of soothing balm, to insist that the UK could cope just fine on its own.

(...)As far as it is possible to tell, there was a collective sharp intake of breath in the aftermath of the vote, but then consumers carried on regardless. The latest monthly <u>health-check</u> of household
40 sentiment found a sharp drop in optimism in July followed by a rapid recovery in August. John Lewis and Next – two <u>bellwethers</u> of activity in the high street – say trading has not been affected by Brexit.

This doesn't mean everything is fine. Britain has deep structural economic problems that would have to be addressed inside or outside the EU. Investment has been weak, productivity has flatlined
45 since the recession, earnings growth is running at half its 4-5% pre-financial crisis level and, except in times of war, the balance of payments deficit has never been higher.

Brexit could make some of these challenges more acute. Investment is likely to remain <u>subdued</u>, while the fall in value of the pound since the referendum will push up inflation by making imports more expensive. That will <u>put the squeeze on</u> consumer spending power.

50 But in other respects, Brexit has been a help. It has forced the government to take a long, hard look at the British economy – something that would not have happened without the shock administered by the referendum. It's brought home the fact that most of Britain feels disconnected from the economic story peddled by successive governments.

For decades, there's been a tendency for businesses to meet rising demand by employing cheap
55 labour rather than by investing in modern equipment. Large chunks of the economy are characterised by low skills, low wages, and low productivity. As the Resolution Foundation noted this week, companies that rely on the ability to import low-cost employees from the EU are going to have to rethink their business models. This is not necessarily a bad thing.

(...)When I voted for Brexit on 23 June, I did so for three reasons: because the European Union is a
60 failed project; because Europe is moving in an increasingly free-market direction; and because I wanted to shake up the status quo. It would take an extremely deep and prolonged recession to make me regret my choice. That prospect seems even <u>more remote</u> than it did eight weeks ago.

(905 words)

I. COMPRÉHENSION

Choisissez la réponse qui vous paraît la plus adéquate en fonction du sens du texte.

1. From line 1 to line 7, it should be understood that:

(A) Brexit has caused disruption in the UK's economy

(B)the government has been trying in vain to sell UK bonds

(C) economists had predicted a drop in retail sales if Brexit won

(D) the dark predictions stopped after the referendum

2. From line 1 to line 7, it should be understood that:

(A) People who voted to remain in the EU expected a recession would prove them right

(B) People thought the state of the economy was terrible before the referendum

(C) People thought the economy would improve after the referendum

(D) The referendum has caused unemployment to rise

3. From line 8 to line 14, it should be understood that:

(A) Companies have had a hard time with credit since the referendum

(B) pension funds and insurance companies have kept buying UK bonds

(C) pension funds and insurance companies have disinvested from the UK

(D) the impact of the referendum on British consumers showed in the summer

4. From line 15 to line 17, it should be understood that:

(A) The referendum result has had a positive effect on employment

(B) The referendum result has had no effect on unemployment

(C) city bosses always see their predictions verified

(D) predictions on the impact of the referendum on unemployment were wrong

5. From line 18 to line 24, it should be understood that:

(A) There is a lot of data suggesting a slowdown of the economy for the second half of 2016

(B) There is a £30 bn hole in the public finances as a result of the referendum

(C) it is too early to be really optimistic about the impact of Brexit on the economy

(D) The UK has had to devise an emergency budget as a result of the referendum

6. From line 25 to line 30, it should be understood that:

(A) Project Fear encouraged businesses to invest before the referendum

(B) economic authorities succeeding in scaring people and businesses about Brexit

(C) economic authorities were in favour of brexit and influenced voters

(D) dire economic consequences have flowed from Brexit

7. From line 31 to line 37, it should be understood that:

(A) the government's objective after the referendum was to shame British people about their vote

(B) All the polls indicated that consumption was going to pick up soon

(C) the government had to rush to fix the negative impact of the scare campaign it had engineered

(D) scare campaigns about recession generally turn out to be self-fulfilling prophecies

8. From line 38 to line 42, it should be understood that:

(A) two major retailers claim trade was not affected by the result of the referendum

(B) two major traders from the City say the stock exchange was not affected by the brexit vote

(C) there was a sharp drop in sales immediately after the referendum but it didn't last

(D) the stock market went south in July but picked up in August

9. From line 43 to line 49, it should be understood that:

(A) brexit could help fix some of the problems inherited from the financial crisis

(B) wages have kept rising at the same rate even after the recession hit

(C) the falling pound will boost purchasing power of imported goods

(D) brexit is likely to compound some of the existing structural problems of the British economy

10. From line 50 to line 53, it should be understood that:

(A) the referendum has forced the government to be more realistic and honest about the economy

(B) the referendum has forced the government to take drastic measures about the economy

(C) people were convinced by the government's economic narrative but still voted leave

(D) brexit was no surprise to the government and they were well prepared to it

11. From line 54 to line 58, it should be understood that:

(A) the British economy has a productivity issue due to low-skilled immigrant workers

(B) one good thing about brexit is that it is going to put an end to immigrant exploitation

(C) the british economy is characterized by a high level of investment in modern equipment

(D) businesses in Britain have faced rising demand since the referendum

12. From line 59 to line 62, it should be understood that:

(A) the writer of this op-ed was very happy with the state of things before the referendum

(B) the writer of this op-ed is in favour of the free-market economy

(C) the writer of this op-ed thinks recession is coming to Britain

(D) the writer of this op-ed thinks he was definitely right in voting for brexit

II. LEXIQUE

Choisissez la réponse qui vous paraît la plus appropriée en fonction du contexte.

(les mots sont soulignés dans le texte)

13. doom and gloom (line 4) means :

(A) depressing news

(B) catastrophic reports

(C) anticipations of disaster

(D) falling interest rates

14. dumping (line 13) means :

(A) selling off

(B) speculating on

(C) driving down the value of

(D) attacking

15. some caveats are in order (line 18) means :

A) some trouble might be brewing

(B) some caution is in order

(C) some optimism is in order

(D) some economic indexes are stable

16. scant (line 18) means :

(A) alarming

(B) being processed

(C) ambiguous

(D) wanting

17. reeling from (line 22) means :

(A) recovering from

(B) resenting

(C) feeling the hurt from

(D) rebelling against

18. it put the wind up (line 25) means :

(A) scared

(B) boosted the morale of

(C) encouraged

(D) put pressure on

18. warier (line 25) means :

(A) more willing

(B) more daring

(C) more cautious

(D) less timorous

19. chill out (line 33) means :

(A) be careful

(B) relax

(C) buy more

(D) save more

20. health-check (line 39) means :

(A) investigation

(B) test

(C) opinion poll

(D) checkup

21. bellwethers (line 41) means :

(A) guides

(B) oracles

(C) experts

(D) traders

22. subdued (line 47) means :

(A) profitable

(B) low

(C) high

(D) risky

23. put the squeeze on (line 49) means :

(A) boost

(B) reduce

(C) send a warning to

(D) put pressure on

24. more remote (line 62) means :

(A) closer

(B) more likely

(C) scarier

(D) more unlikely

III. COMPETENCE GRAMMATICALE

Choisissez la proposition correcte.

25.

(A) low-cost labour has allowed British business to thrive so far

(B) low-cost labour have allowed British businesses to thrive so far

(C) low cost labour has allowed British businesses to thrive so far

(D) low-cost labour has allowed British businesses to thrive so far

26.

(A) The brexit referendum's result has taken the government by surprise

(B) The brexit's referendum's result has taken the government by surprise

(C) The result of the brexit referendum has taken the government by surprise

(D)The result of the brexit's referendum has taken the government by surprise

27.

(A) The referendum has taken place nearly 4 months ago

(B) The referendum has taken place since nearly 4 months

(C) The referendum took place nearly 4 months ago

(D) The referendum has taken place for nearly 4 months

28.

(A) No sooner was the result made official than the pound dropped sharply

(B) No sooner had the result been made official but the pound dropped sharply

(C) No sooner were the result made official than the pound dropped sharply

(D) No sooner has the result been made official than the pound dropped sharply

29.

(A) the voter turnout was high, with less people abstaining than in 1975

(B) the voter turnout was high, with fewer people abstaining than in 1975

(C) voter turnout was high, with less people abstaining than in 1975

(D) voter turnout was high, with fewer people abstaining than in 1975

30.

(A) the turnout among young people was much higher than it had been anticipated

(B) turnout among young people was much higher than it had been anticipated

(C) turnout among young people was much higher than had been anticipated

(D) the turnout among young people was much higher than had been anticipated

31.The refugee crisis influenced the vote. It was...

(A) one crisis too much

(B) one crisis of too much

(C) one too many crises

(D) one crisis too many

32. The referendum has undoubtedly had great bearing on ...

(A) British politic

(B) British politics

(C) British politicos

(D) British pols

33. Experts deem... another referendum will be scheduled

(A) it is likely that

(B) it is as likely that

(C) it likely that

(D) likely that

34. It could take place as soon as the dust... a bit

(A) will settle

(B) will have settled

(C) settles

(D) has settled

35. the result ... different if the financial crisis...

(A) would have been ... hadn't happened

(B) would have been ... didn't happen

(C) would be ... hadn't happened

(D) would be ... didn't happen

36.

(A) The May's Cabinet is only provisional, the Tories will soon elect another leader

(B) May Cabinet is only provisional, the Tories will soon elect another leader

(C) The May Cabinet is only provisional, the Tories will soon elect another leader

(D) May's the Cabinet is only provisional, the Tories will soon elect another leader

37.Senior Tories, many... campaigned for 'Leave', are embarrassed at the result

(A) of which

(B) among which

(C) of whom

(D) of those

38. It is only a few months ... the vote took place but it feels like ages

(A) ago that

(B) since

(C) that

(D) since that

39. Many pessimists reckon the vote will not change...at all

(A) anything

(B) everything

(C) all

(D) a thing

MINES-PONTS Sujet d'entraînement N°1: EXPRESSION ÉCRITE

Baidu uses millions of users' location data to make predictions

By Hal Hodson, *The New Scientist*, 20 July 2016 (adapted)

Baidu, China's internet search giant, has shown just what you can learn when you have access to enough location data.

The firm's Big Data Lab in Beijing has announced that it has used billions of location records from its 600 million users as a lens on the Chinese economy, tracking the flux of people around offices and shops as a proxy measurement for employment and consumption activity. The lab even used the data to predict Apple's second quarter revenue in China.

We already know that location data is useful, tracking population movements and the spread of disease, for example, but this is the first time that a company on the scale of Google, Facebook or Baidu has shown its hand. The data generated by their huge user bases gives these companies enormous power and insight that they don't typically talk about. Academic researchers have great difficulty accessing databases like this. But Baidu can just peer into its own servers. The search giant is saying exactly what it can do with the data, and how much data it has.

First, the researchers hand-labelled thousands of areas of interest – offices, shopping centres and industrial zones – across the country. Then they studied the location data – which runs from the end of 2014 to the middle of 2016 – to see how many people were at those places at each time, and how that changed through the year

Bird's eye view

The data presents a strange bird's eye view of Chinese society. It captures a large shoe factory in south-east China closing down in early 2016 – the area of the factory, once buzzing with location traces, suddenly empty like an abandoned beehive. A few months earlier, a busy mobile phone factory in Jiangsu province, on the east coast, is gutted.

The data also shows success and growth. The number of people going to a software park in Beijing doubles from 2014 to now, while attendance at a start-up's offices skyrockets after it receives investment in mid-2015.

Baidu has collated all the data to build an employment index for China, a number that reflects the overall state of the labour market by tracking how many people are visiting industrial, manufacturing and technology zones in the country. The index shows that employment in manufacturing has dipped by roughly 10 per cent in China since 2014, while high tech employment has grown slightly.

(...)"To the best of our knowledge, we are the first to measure the second largest economy by mining such unprecedentedly large scale and fine granular spatial-temporal data," the Baidu researchers write.

Yves-Alexandre de Montjoye, at Imperial College London's Data Science Institute, says it's good that Baidu is being open about its impressive capabilities.

(...)De Montjoye says one issue still remains – whether we really want just a few large web companies to control the power they wield through this data. "It really asks the question of how can we make this data more available, both in the NHS and Google's case and here," he says. (505 words)

Question 1 : **According to the article, what has Baidu brought to the world of data mining ? Answer the question in your own words. (80 words +/- 10 percent, 4 points)**

Question 2 : **« *one issue still remains – whether we really want just a few large web companies to control the power they wield through this data* ». Comment on this quotation from the article. (180 words +/-10 percent, 8 points)**

MINES- PONTS Sujet d'entraînement N°1 : Thème (8 points)

Bref, voilà pourquoi je me trouvais gare d'Austerlitz (...)J'ai fini par sentir que quelqu'un me tapait sur l'épaule, ça m'a pris un peu de temps parce que j'étais très concentrée, et dans ce cas-là un mammouth pourrait se rouler sur mes baskets, je ne m'en rendrais pas compte. Je me suis retournée.

– T'as pas une clope ?

Elle portait un pantalon kaki sale, un vieux blouson troué aux coudes, une écharpe Benetton comme celle que ma mère garde au fond de son placard en souvenir de quand elle était jeune.

– Non, je suis désolée, je ne fume pas. J'ai des chewing-gums à la menthe, si vous voulez.

Elle a fait la moue, puis m'a tendu la main, je lui ai donné le paquet, elle l'a fourré dans son sac.

"Salut, je m'appelle No. Et toi ?

- No ?

- Oui.

- Moi, c'est Lou... Lou Bertignac (...)

- Je t'ai déjà vue ici, plusieurs fois. Qu'est-ce que tu fais ?

-Je viens pour regarder les gens."

Delphine de Vigan, *No et moi*, 2007

MINES-PONTS Sujet d'entraînement N°2: EXPRESSION ÉCRITE

Europe's net neutrality guidelines seen as a victory for the open web

by Amar Toor Aug 30, 2016, *The Verge* (adapted)

Europe's telecommunications regulator has published final guidelines on how the EU will implement net neutrality rules that were adopted last year, in what digital rights groups are hailing as a victory for the free and open internet. The guidelines, published Tuesday, clarify vaguely worded provisions that experts say could have been exploited by telecoms to favor certain internet services over others.

The net neutrality rules adopted by the European Parliament last year aimed to strengthen net neutrality by requiring internet service providers (ISPs) to treat all web traffic equally, without favoring some services over others. But the regulations contained several loopholes that raised concerns among net neutrality advocates, including a provision that would have allowed ISPs to create "fast lanes" for "specialized services," and another that would have allowed for zero-rating, under which certain services and apps would be exempt from counting against monthly data limits. A "traffic management" provision would have allowed telecoms to prioritize internet traffic from some services over others.

"A TRIUMPH FOR THE EUROPEAN DIGITAL RIGHTS MOVEMENT"

Those provisions were clarified under the guidelines published today by the Body of European Regulators for Electronic Communications (BEREC). "ISPs are prohibited from blocking or slowing down of Internet traffic, except where necessary," BEREC said. "The exceptions are limited to: traffic management to comply with a legal order, to ensure network integrity and security, and to manage congestion, provided that equivalent categories of traffic are treated equally."

The guidelines prohibit zero-rating in circumstances "where all applications are blocked or slowed down once the data cap is reached," though they acknowledge that some cases are "less clear-cut." European regulators should assess such practices on a case-by-case basis, BEREC said, taking account for factors such as the market share of an ISP, effects on app choice, and the scale of the practice. The regulations also allow for traffic management "under limited circumstances;" traffic management practices that block, interfere with, or slow down services and apps would be banned.

The guidelines provide examples of what could be considered as a specialized service, including VoLTE (high-quality voice calls), linear IPTV services, and remote surgeries, which would operate separately from the internet. Such services would have to meet certain quality and capacity requirements to ensure that they can only operate on networks that are not connected to the internet.

Net neutrality advocates welcomed BEREC's guidelines as a milestone for the open internet in Europe. "Europe is now a global standard-setter in the defense of the open, competitive and neutral internet," Joe McNamee, executive director of the Brussels-based organization European Digital Rights (EDRi), said in a statement. Net neutrality activist Thomas Lohninger, of *SaveTheInternet.eu,* described the tougher guidelines as "a triumph for the European digital rights movement." (452 words)

Question 1 : Why are BEREC's guidelines considered a 'triumph' by activists ? (80 words +/- 10 percent)

Question 2 : Do you think net neutrality is important ? Why ? Support your point with relevant examples. (180 words +/- 10 percent)

MINES- PONTS Sujet d'entraînement N°2 : Thème (8 points)

Je donnai un coup de main à ma mère, j'essorai la laitue et préparai la vinaigrette en les écoutant toutes les trois cancaner sur madame Untel qui avait fait un scandale à la pharmacie ou sur monsieur X à qui on avait découvert un cancer de la prostate. Et ma mère qui disait selon le cas : « Elle devrait avoir honte de se comporter comme ça, ça ne se fait pas » ou « C'est quand même malheureux, si jeune... » De mon côté, je restais silencieuse, je détestais ces commérages.

Je le restai tout autant durant le repas, présidé comme toujours par mon père. De temps à autre je jetai un regard à Pierre, qui se sentait comme un poisson dans l'eau au milieu de ma famille, pourtant si ennuyeuse et à l'opposé de mes envies. Pour me distraire, je faisais le service, comme lorsque j'étais la jeune fille de la maison (...) Lorsque je revins à table avec le plateau de fromages, une de mes belles-soeurs m'interpella.

"Iris, ta robe est superbe ! Chez qui l'as-tu trouvée ?"

Je lui souris et je sentis enfin le regard de Pierre sur moi.

"Elle vient de mon grenier."

Agnès Martin Lugand, *Entre mes mains le bonheur se faufile*, **2014**

MINES-PONTS Sujet d'entraînement N°3: EXPRESSION ÉCRITE

What About the Planet?

Paul Krugman, *The New York Times*, October 7, 2016

Our two major political parties are at odds on many issues, but nowhere is the gap bigger or more consequential than on climate.

If Hillary Clinton wins, she will move forward with the Obama administration's combination of domestic clean-energy policies and international negotiation — a one-two punch that offers some hope of reining in greenhouse gas emissions before climate change turns into climate catastrophe.

If Donald Trump wins, the paranoid style in climate politics — the belief that global warming is a hoax perpetrated by a vast international conspiracy of scientists — will become official doctrine, and catastrophe will become all but inevitable.

So why does the media seem so determined to ignore this issue? Why, in particular, does it almost seem as if there's a rule against bringing it up in debates?

Before I get there, a brief summary of the policy divide.

It's strange how little credit the Obama administration gets for its environmental policies.

Everyone has heard about how loan guarantees to one solar-energy company, Solyndra, went sour — at a cost, by the way, that amounted to only a bit more than half the amount Mr. Trump personally lost in just one year thanks to bad business decisions. Few people, by contrast, have heard about the green energy revolution that the administration's loans and other policy support helped promote, with plunging prices and soaring consumption of solar and wind power.

Nor have many heard about the administration's tightening of fuel efficiency standards, especially for trucks and buses, which in itself is one of the most significant environmental moves in decades.

And if Mrs. Clinton wins, it's more or less certain that the biggest moves yet — the Clean Power Plan, which would regulate emissions from power plants, and the Paris climate agreement, which commits all of the world's major economies to make significant emission cuts — will become reality.

Meanwhile, there's Mr. Trump, who has repeatedly called climate change a hoax and has suggested that it was invented by China to hurt U.S. competitiveness. I wish I could say that this puts him outside the mainstream of his party, but it doesn't.

So there is a huge, incredibly consequential divide on climate policy. Not only is there a vast gap between the parties and their candidates, but this gap arguably matters more for the future than any of their other disagreements. So why don't we hear more about it?(...)
(402 words)

Question 1 : Why does Paul Krugman suggest the US media is acting irresponsibly in this campaign ? (80 words +/- 10 percent, 4 points)

Question 2 : Can politics impact global warming ? Illustrate your answer with relevant examples (180 words +/- 10 percent, 8 points)

MINES- PONTS - Sujet d'entraînement N°3 : Thème (8 points)

Elle était très en forme et m'avait donné rendez-vous dans un café du 1er arrondissement, un de ces somptueux établissements auxquels l'affluence de touristes, seigneurs du lieu, confère un air décadent qui lui plaisait. Elle a très vite insisté pour que nous nous promenions, malgré la bruine, ce qui m'a contrarié, je n'avais aucune envie de jouer les vacanciers par un après-midi d'automne humide et froid, mais elle débordait d'énergie et a fini par me convaincre.(...)

– Tu sais Franz, m'a-t-elle dit au moment où nous longions les files de calèches au bord de la place Saint-Stéphane, il y a quelque chose de très intéressant chez ceux qui pensent que Vienne est la porte de l'Orient, ce qui m'a fait rire à mon tour.

– Non non, ne rigole pas, je pense que je vais écrire là-dessus, sur les représentations de Vienne en *Porta Orientis (1).*

(1) Ne pas traduire

Mathias Enard, Boussole, 2015

CORRIGÉS
des sujets d'entraînement

CORRIGÉ SUJET X-ENS N°1: SYNTHÈSE

Pokémon Go, harbinger of a « Brave New Augmented World »?

From its astronomically successful debut in July Pokémon Go has divided expert opinion, yet there is a point of near-universal agreement: the game has caused Augmented Reality to go mainstream, signalling change for us all. What sort of world is Pokémon Go heralding, and for whose benefit? According to blogger A.M Jacob in his October 2016 *Synthesis* entry, Augmented Reality opens Frontier-like vistas of opportunities. This positive augmentation is confirmed by two charts from T*he Independent* and 7Park Data in July. The same month, A. Hern takes a sterner view in *The Guardian*: Pokémon G is raising concerns of privacy, property and decency requiring legislative action ; to his *Guardian* colleague S. Horvat, the 'massification' of AR points at the building of a monopoly on our reality, controlled by Silicon Valley and the US government. These papers discuss the nature and scope of the « augmentation », the issue of private space v. public space, and ultimately that of the common interest v. private interests.

According to Jacob,   AR is thrilling because augmentation happens in quantitative as well as qualitative terms: AR multiplies spaces *ad infinitum*. The augmentation is materialized in statistics : The two charts show that the game has tremendously increased both the time users stay connected and potential benefits for their health. This is a paradoxical effect, but it signals momentous changes in our lifestyles and environment, and not only for the better, in Horvat's view : Silicon Valley has undertaken to colonize our reality, and changing the way it looks is only one of elements in the strategy. To Hern, the colonization of space is already palpable in the form of an invasion of privacy and property by « Pokémon trainers » attracted to virtual spots that turn out to be real-life places where they cause disturbances. Niantic, the developer, has been in trouble before for inappropriately locating its virtual hotspots in places of memory such as Auschwitz.

Accordingly, Hern calls for collective state-enforced legal protection of privacy and property, similar to that of airspace, but Jacob doubts the efficiency of this in view of the formidable drive for profit which AR will fuel ; the charts showing the unprecedented leap in connection time and the ability of Pokémon Go to entice people to walk for miles and hit designated spots, do suggest that AR has started an advertisers' gold rush. For Jacob, Silicon Valley has reopened prospects reminiscent of the 19th century Drive Westward, when the land belonged to the daring pioneer. However, all three writers agree that control of the phenomenon will happen in the long run, although they have a different perspective on that control.

To Hern, after the improvisation phase (with Niantic fixing privacy, property and safety issues in piecemeal fashion to avoid litigation), the law will catch up and provide blanket protection. Jacob reckons that most users being reasonable and pragmatic, AR is likely to grow self-regulated though market forces; its most useful applications will be regrouped for the better; monopoly of the fittest through judicious acquisition of the best technology is no evil, claims Palantir's Thiel quoted by Horvat, who for his part strongly objects : the advent of AR is the result of corporate-and-tech concentration that masks even more sinister designs ; it was made possible by the Google location-data technology which is a military-capitalist joint venture involving robber barons rather than heroic pioneers. Moreover, massive state surveillance and control are looming behind Pokémon Go, a harbinger of the complete integration of our environment within « the internet of things » ; in this dystopian nightmare scenario, everything about and around us will be centralized in a giant computer system.

Jacob and Hern are optimistic : regulation, either imposed or natural, will happen, and Jacob even suggests that AR will favour collaborative interaction. On the other hand, Horvat sees our reality being altered in view of a takeover by special interests. In these early days of mass AR, views are extremely polarized. (674 words)

CORRIGÉ SUJET X-ENS N°1: TEXTE D'OPINION

Solipsism is the notion that only one's mind is sure to exist, the rest of the world, including other minds, being hypothetical. Is Augmented Reality going to compound the solipsistic tendencies in individuals and groups which social media has already encouraged ? In my view, *Guardian* columnist Hari Kunzru may be very insightful when he raises the social and political implications of tech-induced bigotry, however, in some respects he mistakes consequences for causes.

Kunzru is concerned that, although current AR apps are fairly harmless or even useful, the potential for tailored realities they hold is likely to encourage escapism and unsociability. People may be tempted to wipe out those intractable aspects of « real real » that are actually good for them. I fully subscribe to this criticism. As Montaigne wrote , we should, for our own good, « seek the infection of an unknown air » : it is by confronting what resists or offends us in the real world, that we grow up, learn to make concessions, take distance with our beliefs, and adjust to a reality that was not created just for us. Our shared reality is better for us than augmented reality.

Kunzru mentions relevant research on the way opinions solidify to become entrenched certainties, a phenomenon dubbed « the confirmation bias ». People tend to seek the like-minded, both online and in their environment (Americans now even pick neighbourhoods where residents are likely to share their political views). This is the recipe for self-righteousness and intolerance, materialized in the strident, populist and extremist turn US politics has recently taken. Like the writer, I am worried at the disappearance of that « common ground » of democratic politics, that « agora » where debate happens, concessions are made, and consensus sometimes achieved ; besides, will the shared space of civilized social interaction vanish too as AR becomes a part of our lives ?

This would imply that tech has the capacity profoundly to alter the structure of our polities and societies, which is where I disagree with the writer. I believe that tech is an epitome of our world, not a root cause, an agent, not an engine. It was not the internet that changed things, it was the use we made of it, the way in which social media and alternative news sources emerged ; these reflected the culture of our times as much as they amplified it. Individualism, globalization, secularization, consumerism, among other things which predated the Net, have contributed to the vanishing of the relative consensus found in western countries for most of the 20th century

Moreover,   this consensus maybe never existed ; it is just that before the internet wave, communication was top-down and unilateral – from the establishment to ordinary people via the media and the dominant culture, not the other way round ; the « filter bubble » was the illusion that the establishment represented the majority; whereas today communication is horizontal and multilateral, therefore monopolies on speech and thought are challenged. Communication technologies and the choice of sources have empowered ordinary people and enabled them to create their own « filter bubbles » and « illusions of the majority ». This inevitably produces mutual alienation, tensions, polarization, which apparently threaten both political and social stability.

However, this is a transition phase, and I do think social/political consensus will take shape again in time, along new lines. The same goes for AR, which after a period of relative anarchy will probably end up bringing people together and serving the common interest rather than favouring a form of social separatism. (599 words)

US : Solar is taking off, but the sky is overcast

The success of solar energy suggests it is coming of age in the US, yet it is also experiencing growing pains. Is the solar deployment now happening, technically   and economically premature ?   M. Weiser's June 28 piece in *The Guardian* shows that solar energy is growing exponentially in the US, thanks in part to falling costs ; this is corroborated by two charts from *The Guardian* and *The Scientific American*; however, this boom is threatened by complicated subsidies and billing issues, as well as technological hurdles detailed in an article by N. Stauffer from the *MITEI* in 2015 ; one problem is the intermittent nature of insolation, and Tesla CEO's response to this is a plan to develop energy storage technology, as *The New York Times* reports in August 2016 ; but the third chart from *Bloomberg* confirms the financial world's misgivings about his vision.

The articles and charts all document something like the beginning of an energy transition in the US, driven by the expansion of home and business solar panels. Chart 1 shows an almost 100 % increase from 2015 to 2016 ; with thousands of new installations every year, solar is turning into a full-blown, job-creating industry, *The Guardian* underlines, even if it only accounts for less than 1% of all electricity production ; this is still provided by natural gas, coal and nuclear plants, as explained by Stauffer, but solar tops them all in terms of new installations and new megawatts added. This growth has prompted SolarCity to build a large manufacturing facility for panels in NY state, and other companies are following suit to answer domestic demand.

As *The NYT* reports, Mr Musk, owner of heavily indebted SolarCity banks on the falling costs of solar hardware, which has boosted demand lately ; indeed chart 2 shows cost per watt of installation to have been almost divided by two since 2010 ; solar energy also benefits from lavish subsidies, according to *The NYT* and *The Guardian* ; the latter points out the very enticing fiscal incentives for private owners and businesses who « go solar »

However, precisely because of this success, solar power is running into structural difficulties and oppositions described in all four documents. The paradox of clean and sustainable energy is that the more of it there is, the more demand on alternative provision of energy grows, as a professor quoted by Stauffer, and *The Guardian,* explain. Solar power is an on/off source, and more solar-powered homes and electric cars means more demand when the sun isn't there. This puts enormous pressure on existing facilities in two ways : the electricity grid has to absorb the solar power produced by home and business installations, and quickly meet increased demand when there is no insolation. It all comes with a cost.

Hence the resistance of the local energy industry, described in an example given by *The Guardian* : solar is expanding at the expense of the whole sector's profitability, and energy companies are challenging its privileges at state level. Besides, Stauffer underlines, home and business owners who feed solar energy into the grid are getting less and less return on their investment : the more solar power there is, the cheaper it is, whereas the price of other energies is high. This might be the reason why the market is slowing down, and SolarCity's shares are going south in spite of Elon Musk's optimism. His answer to all these issues is technology : the synergy between Tesla and SolarCity will make it possible soon to develop energy storage technology to relieve the pressure on the grid, attract more customers to solar power and save money for the two companies, *The NYT* reports. Soon, however, is not soon enough for Wall Street, where some skepticism is being voiced regarding Mr Musk's grand project *'to accelerate the advent of a sustainable-energy world.'* (657 words title included)

CORRIGÉ SUJET X-ENS N°2: TEXTE D'OPINION

Decades ago, the French Annales School popularized the importance of long-term trends and social phenomena in history, and relativised the importance of political events and individual figures ; yet we still like to think that a single man can make history ; at least this seems to be the viewpoint of Anna Wittwer, author of a recent op-ed on the *Synthesis* tech blog about visionary American entrepreneurs Elon Musk and Mark Zuckerberg's 'solar epic'. I propose to discuss what she argues these men's contribution to the world could be, and to offer some criticism of her hero worship : it doesn't do justice to a collective effort towards the advent of cleaner, renewable energy for all. Finally, I reckon philanthropy has little to do with it.

Facebook wants to bring internet to the whole world thanks to a solar-powered drone, and Elon Musk intends to stock-merge Tesla motors with SolarCity in order to develop solar energy storage and accelerate solar penetration in the US. Both men intend to speed up the advent of a fossil-fuel-free world, and Ms Wittwer deplores the obstruction they are facing, in particular Mr Musk, who risks bankruptcy, and also the fact that the electricity industry is beginning to put legal hurdles in the path of a booming solar market in the US. The energy transition revolution that is going to liberate us, like Icarus from gravity, is supposedly under way, but financiers and lobbyists might nail us to the ground.

This view overlooks the collective effort that got America where it is (the country is the 5th world producer of solar panels, US solar energy creates more 'new' megawatts than fossil fuels). Musk and Zuckerberg are riding a wave they didn't initiate, and which had a cost : solar energy is heavily subsidized. Fiscal incentives for those who instal it mean that the taxpayers as a whole are paying for it. Given the electricity billing system, those without solar have been, are, and will be footing the bill for those who have it : the cost of infrastructure adjustment to absorb solar energy into the grid and to pay for it is being borne by the existing power plants and utilities, and ultimately by the consumer who is on regular energy. It also harms the industry's profitability, and all in all it is unfair because it is already well-off people who are on solar. I think both the industry and the American people as a whole should be given their due in terms of recognition for the achievements of solar power : it is a collective effort. Someone is also paying for Tesla's and SolarCity's abysmal debts, and deserves credit as well.

Moreover, meritorious though it may seem for those two innovating CEOs to work at 'accelerating' history, philanthropy is not necessarily what drives them. Self-interest and self-aggrandizement also come into the mix. Aquila would ensure that no one escapes Facebook, and the project seems to involve captive markets, as access to only some internet services will be possible.

As to our liberation from the energy sector's hegemony thanks to solar autonomy which Ms Wittwer envisions, I dont believe in it : there could also be monopolies of various natures on solar power. There is no reason to believe that it would be preserved from multinational, or local control. (550 words)

CORRIGÉ SUJET CENTRALE-SUPÉLEC N° 1

Satire, the gadfly (1) of democracy

'A *true gentleman never hurt anyone's feelings unintentionally*', Oscar Wilde wrote, encapsulating the very spirit of satire. Satire hurts intentionally, it harms ignorance and bigotry, which is why it should be valued, according to Howard Jacobson in *The Independent* in October 2015 ; George Orwell's introduction to his 1945 satirical novel *Animal Farm* goes further: excessive regard for the political 'orthodoxy' of the moment could lead to totalitarianism, something which the January 2015 cartoon by Gee also suggests. For NY times pundit D. Brooks writing about the Charlie Hebdo attack in 2015, society can deal with satirical outrage without resorting to censorship. **These documents point out that even sound democracies sometimes suppress criticism; they also suggest why and how, on the contrary, democracy should seek to accommodate satire at all cost.**

The columnists and cartoonist are reacting to free speech controversies, Charlie Hebdo for Brooks and Gee, and anti-transgender comments for Jacobson, and they all use this to criticize the devastation of political correctness in their respective countries. Brooks remarks that unorthodox opinions, such as religious or anti-gun views, are *de facto* censured on US campuses, even though the principle of free speech itself is championed : they supported the French satirists but would probably have found ways to bar their opinions at home. There is no official censorship, but local or national 'orthodoxies' are at work to make sure that nonconform expression is not heard ; for instance controversial speakers' lectures are cancelled, or, as Orwell points out, the whole establishment exerts tacit pressure against the publicization of politically incorrect views, like his own when he satirized Stalin's totalitarian USSR. Censorship is internalized by the media, writers, but also the ignorant public, Jacobson remarks. The internet crowd in Britain fail to grasp the subtlety of British intellectual snobbery, exemplified in novelist Martin Amis's lampooning of J. Corbyn. Jacobson and Brooks contend that people' s taking issue with satire prove that they are the butt of it, and that it is therefore useful : it shakes us out of our complacency, targetting people who cannot take distance with their creeds ; this is what the cartoon means, showing satire to be irresistible in spite of repression.

Satirists are not necessarily accurate or subtle, Brooks goes on to explain, and Jacobson remarks that they needn't even send a relevant message, an opinion also found in Orwell : that a satirist's views should prove right or wrong is not the issue, and the subversive smiley in the cartoon is a case in point. What matters to uphold the old democratic tradition, to Orwell, is diversity and a critical sense, instead of political opportunism or cowardice, and again, the cartoon is a clear illustration of this ; For Brooks, society doesn't need laws to discriminate the value of opinions expressed, therefore the candid, outrageous satirist should be allowed to say that 'the emperor has no clothes'. All writers agree that a democratic society implies debate, concessions, and the acceptance of other people's free opinions. It is impoverished when one speech is suppressed because it offends. If there is a limit to it for Orwell and Jacobson, it is that of violence or visible harm an opinion can cause. To Brooks, the judgment of society is protection enough. (550 words title included)

(1)Gadfly *(social), a person who upsets the status quo, who stimulates or annoys especially by persistent criticism*

CORRIGÉ SUJET CENTRALE-SUPÉLEC N° 2

Soccer : a way of life and an art for some, a waste of everything for others

Football fans have a hard time getting across to non-fans their love for a team. What can explain such devotion, which also elicits scorn? In 1991 British Author Nick Hornby attempted to rationalize his passion in the novel *Fever Pitch*, and there are also some clues in specialist Ed Smith who pays tribute to Arsenal's Wenger's coaching style in *The Independent* (December 2015) ; A collection of posters of Manchester United's 1990s hero Cantona shows that dedication borders on idolatry ; those three documents would probably be lost on Stephen Moore, an American columnist who expresses bafflement at the passion for soccer in *The Daily Signal* in June 2014. How comprehensible are British football fanaticism and the corresponding annoyance at it ?

In the introduction to his novel, Hornby describes an obsession which has him constantly remembering football moves in the middle of his daily routine, and more : he has spent his adult life finding analogies with soccer in everything else, making it the focus of the world ; Manchester United fans' imagination works along similar lines in the posters : Cantona is substituted to the monarch, and even to God, and his birthdate is even inscribed in British history. This excess is exactly what irks Moore, looking at the global hype about the World Cup in 2014 : soccer everywhere, except in the US, which performs poorly in the game. This is only normal, he contends, because soccer is unexciting. Scores are structurally low, when there are 'too many' goals, it kills the game, and this tends to turn soccer into playacting for penalties. It is a terrible waste of talent, energy and time, he argues from an unashamed American productivist point of view. American football, at least, produces results, and some action follows goals ; however, it seems the score isn't what matters either to Hornby or to Smith : the latter explains that the beauty of Arsène Wenger's coachmanship is that he takes his time to build success, and success isn't necessarily about scoring or even winning. There lies the big misunderstanding between Americans and soccer fans everywhere else. Soccer is about entertainment, Smith agrees, but that entertainment is made of many ingredients. A coach's patient, compassionate leadership is one of them ; to Hornby, the beautiful gestures and moves that are a part of his life are more important than titles won. And the legend of Cantona is itself a part of the fun: There is love and myth-making in soccer, that is what fans enjoy too ; no doubt but Wenger will have his share of this love and mythology as well.

All the documents converge on one line: soccer and American football are about more than sport. X admits that it boosts the nation's morale at a time of historical low. To Hornby, soccer says a lot about contemporary society ; the posters bear him out: tradition, institutions, religion are displaced by folk heroes like footballers. Smith, for his part, is very positive about football coaching, the kind of extensive lessons that can be drawn from it about leadership and teaching, about how training to improve rather than exploit pays off in the long run. (550 words title included)

CORRIGÉ SUJET CENTRALE-SUPÉLEC N° 3

Tech-related *angst*

In history, humanity has gone through a number of technological revolutions which have fostered positive change but also caused a great deal of anxiety. This is especially true of Information and Communication Technology. The set of documents focuses on various syndromes induced by tech, and on how to handle them. Romain Dillet from *TechCrunch* offers an assessment of the wariness that seizes the tech media people at the end of an innovation cycle ; too much ICT use can lead to insanity, the cartoon from *Cartoonaday* shows, and in hhis short story *The Murderer*, sci-fi author Ray Bradbury also anticipates on the madness of the 'tyranny of communication' ; in a November 2015 op-ed, *Guardian* columnist Suzanne Moore deals with this tyranny in social media, but in order to relativise it.

Although published in 1953, Bradbury's story conjures up a world very like ours now, where ICT and noise are omnipresent, forcing themselves on people. The hero, Brock, has been put in an asylum for destroying devices like phones and FM systems which he deems hostile; insanity caused by 'machines that yak yak yak' is also the theme of the cartoon which shows a millenial talking nonsense laced with tech gibberish, into his shoe ; he is sitting on top a heap of discarded devices, while a psychiatrist diagnoses him with 'tech fatigue'. The cartoon character's jargon is reminiscent of tech expert Dillet who admits he is suffering from a fatigue syndrome, wanting at times to quit the job because he feels that many promising innovations have turned out to be just nonsensical buzzwords.

He is writing in April 2016 after a number of US tech events when, he claims, he realized that nothing really new or truly useful or exciting was up : new features are copycats, new pitches have a bright future behind them. This causes anxiety about losing his zest and his flair. Anxiety is also central to Moore's survey of the social media detox phenomenon. It appears from studies she mentions that withdrawal from Facebook relieves stress, and she knows people who worry at their progeny's being so hooked on cell phones. A guilty trend has developed regarding social media apps, because the life on them is supposedly the opposite of real life with its genuine personal and spiritual connections, that we miss out on.

Rubbish, says Moore. Social media is not compulsory, it is an addition to life, not an addiction, and Dillet does admit that tech, well understood, is also a wonderful contribution to progress ; to regain faith, one should just learn to sort out the real innovation from the scam. However, Bradbury suggests that the sage in his story is really Brock, who aspires to silence and wants to end the pollution of noise, and the   individual's enslavement to useless communication. The world is mad, not he, but the story is unconclusive as to the possibility of escape. Moore does also admit that detox for a while is all right for some, but she shows that people who claim their real world is different from Facebook are just striking a pose.

The bottom line for Moore and Dillet is that tech can be handled, while Bradbury is pessimistic. But then Bradbury's line was science fiction, not social science. *(548 words title included)*

CORRIGÉ CCP- e3a N° 1: Synthèse

The potential of virtual reality for real humanity

Should we feel upbeat or depressed about the advent of Virtual Reality, materialized in its undeniable mass commercial success in 2016? The articles of the set, all published in that same year, are indeed rather divided on the issue. Documents 1 and 2, from *The Guardian* show the promises VR holds for human cooperation and individual improvement, whereas document 3, from *The Guardian,* questions the potential of VR for human intercourse, and document 4, from the *New York Times*, suggests virtual activities may thwart the development of teenagers into full-grown adults. (*99 words with title*)

Immersion in 3D environments can lead to a broad variety of experiences. With the proper headset and app, millions of doctors worldwide will soon be able to share enhanced experiences of their practice, which is invaluable for peers and students, document 1 explains. This is likely to create the kind of community which the author of document 3 is calling for : what are virtual spaces, even   spectacular ones, if we cannot commune with others in them, she asks ? The question is caused by her encounter with a lonely teen in a Virtual Reality game ; but some people have opposite views of what VR is for. Instead of connecting with the world, an app created by LA guru Chopra will soon enable the user to withdraw from it, which is the point of buddhist meditation : in document 2, he claims that the material world is an illusion, and VR can make this solipsistic claim perceptible to the senses too. R. Douthat, who authored document 4, is for his part very skeptical as to the positive potential of VR, an industry which he claims, is mostly devoted to pornography and games. It's not only 3D, it's the whole virtual dimension of ITC which has changed the younger generations, and not necessrily for the better. Virtual Reality leads to narcissim, isolation, and alienation from what makes adult life worth living : work, intercourse, family.

From these diverging viewpoints, there emerges the sense that VR is what authors make of it according to their own priority focus : A fantastic opportunity to connect with people we would never meet or sympathise with in our ordinary environments, a tool to build collective efforts with a view to helping humanity as a whole, a help to reflect on the primacy of the mind over matter, or on the contrary another agency of destruction of the social fabric as we've known it. (421 words title included)

CORRIGÉ CCP- e3a N° 1: QCM

Rappel du barème :

Bonne réponse= +3

mauvaise réponse= -1

pas de réponse ou réponses multiples = 0

Pour calculer votre note finale de QCM sur 20 vous devez donc diviser votre total de points de COMPREHENSION par 3,6, celui de LEXIQUE par 7,2 et celui de COMPETENCE GRAMMATICALE par 9, puis faire la somme de ces trois résultats.

I. COMPREHENSION

1. From line 1 to line 5 (paragraph 1), it should be understood that:

(B) we use our smartphones at least 200 times a day

2. From line 6 to line 9 (paragraph 2), it should be understood

that: **(A)** **_connectivity may have a bad influence on the way our brain works_**

3. From line 10 to line 14 (paragraph 3), it should be understood

that:**(B)** **_the speed of internet exchanges triggers reflex rather than rational responses_**

4. From line 15 to line 20 (paragraph 4), it should be understood

that:**(C)** **_the inventor of the internet is worried at the turn social media is taking_**

5. From line 21 to line 25 (paragraphs 5 &6) , it should be understood

that:**C)** **_Internet-savvy people would like to see a different kind of internet_**

6. From line 26 to line 32 (paragraph 7), it should be understood

that:**(C)** **_aggressive response is natural to the way our brain works_**

7. From line 33 to line 36 (paragraph 8), it should be understood

that:**(D)** **_the writer wishes people would use System 2 thinking more when interacting on social_** *media*

8. From line 37 to line 41 (paragraph 9), it should be understood

that:**(A)** ***System 1 thinking relies on imperfect knowledge***

9. From line 42 to line 47 (paragraph 10), it should be understood

that:**(D)** *our smartphone responses are often simplistic and therefore inaccurate*

10. From line 48 to line 50 (paragraph 11), it should be understood

that:**(C)** ***System 1 thinking encourages misogynistic comments***

11. From line 51 to line 57 (paragraph 12), it should be understood

that:**(A)** ***the very reason why we surf the net is our preference for System 1 thinking***

12. From line 58 to line 61 (paragraph 13), it should be understood

that: *(C) the writer has doubts about the business future of a social media requiring time*

II. LEXIQUE

13. outweighs (line 7) means :

(D)*exceeds*

14. stock (line 12) means :

(A)*usual*

15. gut reactions (line 12) means :

(B) *emotional responses*

16. went out of his way (line 15) means :

(D) *gave himself great pains*

17. bullying (line 16) means :

(A)*verbal intimidation*

18. marshal (line 33) means :

(C) *organize*

18. hurly-burly (line 36) means :

(A)*tumult*

19. biases (line 37) means :

(C) *distortions*

20. to come up with (line 43) means :

(A) *find*

21. snap (line 45) means :

(D) *hasty*

22. idiosyncratic (line 55) means :

(B) *very original*

23. trivia (line 57) means :

(C) *inessential facts*

24. heeded (line 58) means :

(A) *heard*

III. COMPETENCE GRAMMATICALE

25.

(A) *The people whose posts we respond to on social media*

26.

(A) *I am not used to going on Facebook*

27.

(D) *Instant messaging demands that she respond with the speed of lightning*

28.

(C) ***This 3D headset cost me a week's wages***

29.

(A) ***Social media with heart is the lesser of two evils***

30.

(B) ***Pokémon Go came out last July***

31.

(D) ***No sooner did it come out than millions of 'trainers' started roaming the streets***

32. If you want to tweet, you … better get ready for some bullying

(C) ***had***

33. Not everybody on Facebook gets … posts and pictures shared

(C) ***their***

34. Martha Lane Fox is … Tim Berners-Lee on the necessity to make internet more humane

(A) ***of the same mind as***

35. The Facebook interface is more flexible and interactive than … Twitter

(C) ***that of***

36. Connecting or not connecting is...

(B) _**any user's choice**_

37. in terms of social network innnovation, no one knows what the future may

(A) _**hold**_

38. The … users, the … the fun

(B) _**more… greater**_

39. … Google … launched

(C) _**It's been 18 years since…was**_

CORRIGÉ CCP- e3a N° 2: Synthèse

Water : an old issue and fresh crises

The control and distribution of water has historically been critical. Document 1, a book review from *The New Scientist* in August 2016 describes water control as a part of the art of governance ; document 2 from *ProPublica* in June 2015 and Document 3 from *The Guardian* in June 2016, show the American West undergoing a major water crisis, while millions of Americans across the country risk lead poisoning. Document 4, a 2013 World Resources Institute map, is evidence of high levels of water stress in the world. Is all this about management, or mismanagement of water ?

Water stress happens when the ratio water used/resources is too high, and document 4 shows medium to high stress in China and the US in 2013 ; since then, the California drought and Colorado basin crisis have made things worse in America, with 40 million people facing a crisis, and a potential agricultural catastrophe, as per document 2 ; according to Document, China also has to deal with a drying Yellow River. Millions undergo shortages in the US, and this is worsened by awful management of water distribution : neglected infrastructure has resulted in people being exposed to unacceptable levels of lead in their drinking water, Document 3 explains, and federal laws are powerless : too little is done to coerce private providers.

Climate change isn't to blame for the droughts, natural variance is at play, but document 2 details how the American crisis is attributable to ill-use, to waste, and to an unrealistic appraisal of the resource: People claim more than the Colorado river provides, and there is no water left for Mexico. Will this lead to « water wars », document 1 asks ? The map on document 4 shows a majority of countries suffering at least medium water stress, with Central and Eastern Asia, and the Middle East having high to very high stress : a recipe for tensions ? As per document 1, in history water stress has led to mighty efforts rather than war ; water management was the key to China's successful dynasties, and today the huge canals from the Yangtze to the Yellow river prove that China is aware its future lies in water management ; the history of the Colorado exhibits collaboration, patient negotiation and compromise, which are now being renewed in an effort to save and better use water in the American West. Likewise, document 3 shows a push since 2015 for quality improvement of tap water, under the pressure of the law and the outrage from the Flint scandal. (435 words title included)

CORRIGÉ CCP- e3a N° 2: QCM

I. COMPREHENSION

1. From line 1 to line 4, it should be understood that:

(B) showing such violence against black people on TV is like broadcasting X-rated films

2. From line 5 to line 8, it should be understood that:

(B) the riots and protests are a response to an epidemic of police shootings

3. From line 9 to line 12, it should be understood that:

(C) protesters are angry at the whole system rather than at individual deaths

4. From line 13 to line 16, it should be understood that:

(D) videos now offer evidence of what people used to know by word of mouth only

5. From line 17 to line 20, it should be understood that:

(A) it is no longer possible to stop Black America from defending itself

6. From line 21 to line 26 it should be understood that:

(C) the public should focus on general root causes rather than individual motives

7. From line 26 to line 32, it should be understood that:

(A) the backdrop of indiscriminate police shootings of blacks is structural inequality

8. From line 33 to line 41, it should be understood that:

(B) the question of choice has been displaced by the media rhetoric

9. From line 42 to line 45, it should be understood that:

(B) punishment by law adds to the woes of people living in crime-ridden areas

10. From line 46 to line 49, it should be understood that:

(C) blacks are suspected of crime by association and punished even when innocent

11. From line 50 to line 54, it should be understood that:

(A) unjustified killings are produced by a culture, not just individual officers

12. From line 55 to line 63, it should be understood that:

(C) America as a whole is responsible for the shooting deaths of innocents

II. LEXIQUE

13. stanch (line 8) means

(C) stop

14. turmoil (line 9) means

(A) unrest

15. discrete (line 8) means

(C) disconnected

16. shroud (line 13) means

(C) veil

17. buttressed(line 16) means

(D) reinforced

18. era (line 21) means

(A) time

18. flee (line 25) means

(B) run

19. blight (line 29) means

(D) curse

20. sticky (line 31) means

(C) enduring

21. flight (line 37) means

(A*) departure*

22. poor (line 41) means

(C) ill-advised

23. compounding (line 45) means

(A*) adding to*

24. harbour (line 51) means

(D)exhibit

III. COMPETENCE GRAMMATICALE

25.

(C) Blacks are twice as likely as whites to be pulled over by the road police

26.

(A) To this day official homicide rates by the police in the US have never been disclosed

27.

(C) The Obama administration's record in terms of racial equality is poor

28.

(D) Equal justice is a defining issue of America's

29.

(B) The incarceration rate of blacks is 6 times that of whites

30.

(C) The US is one of the few truly multicultural countries of the world

31.

(A) civil rights have been the centerpiece of the Democrats' agenda since the 1960s

32.

(B) Not everybody can live in crime-free, affluent neighborhoods

33. This is the magistrate … they appointed as prosecutor in the case.

(C) whom

34. They are investigating the scene of the shooting, and all the circumstances...

(A) thereof

35. In many cases, unfortunately, circumstances are... clear

(D) all but

36. Unsatisfactory …, the grand jury's decision is final

(D) though it may be

37. Civil rights groups... some community building in order to prevent those shootings

(A) have been attempting

38. The whole report on the investigation… in … of the New York Times

(C) was published... yesterday's edition ...

39. They will disclose the circumstances as soon as...

(A) *those are known*

CORRIGÉ CCP- e3a N° 3: Synthèse

US, China and climate change : a historical pledge

2016 could go down in history as a turning-point in the fight against climate change, all 3 documents of the set converge on that point. Document one, from Columbia University in December 2015, details the US's plan to cut its emissions ; Document 2, an article from *The Guardian* in July 2016 announces that China's coal use has already peaked ; this probably made it easier for China to ratify the COP 21 agreement along with the US in September, an event commented on in document 3, from the AFP. These documents look at how we got there, and how those countries intend to help stem global warming.

Document 3 reports that in September 2016, two of the world's biggest emitters of carbon ratified the Paris agreements, a step forward in the fight against climate change ; the agreements aim at keeping global temperature rise below 2 degrees Celsius. China has pledged to cut its emissions by around 60 percent below 2005 levels by 2030, and the US has committed to cut its own by around 27 percent by 2025. In July, as per document 2, came a sign that China was likely to meet its targets, when it was announced that its coal use peaked in 2014, earlier than expected. This is a symptom that China is experiencing change, under the pressure of domestic public opinion, environmental concerns about water resources, and a sense of global responsibility. Although a slowing growth may account for the decline in coal use, the latter looks like a long-term trend. This is good news for economists and environmentalists for whom, according to document 2, coal must go if we are to curb global warming.

In the US they are aware of this, according to document 1 : the focus of the nation in order to cut emissions is on better management of electricity production, which uses a lot of coal. But efforts will also have to be made in transportation, and the construction and electrical appliance sectors ; the US has also pledged to help nations fight climate change and alleviate its effects. Both China and the US aim to increase the share of renewable energies in their grids.

Some environmentalists are saying this is only a timid beginning, not the final seal, document 3 underlines. Besides, the US is facing predictable obstruction from vested interests at congressional and local levels, according to document 1. However, this joint commitment on part of China and the US should be hailed, as it is likely to have a considerable influence on the rest of the world. (440 words title included)

CORRIGÉ CCP- e3a N° 3: QCM

I. COMPRÉHENSION

1. From line 1 to line 7, it should be understood that:

(C) economists had predicted a drop in retail sales if Brexit won

2. From line 1 to line 7, it should be understood that:

(A) People who voted to remain in the EU expected a recession would prove them right

3. From line 8 to line 14, it should be understood that:

(B) pension funds and insurance companies have kept buying UK bonds

4. From line 15 to line 17, it should be understood that:

(D) predictions on the impact of the referendum on unemployment were wrong

5. From line 18 to line 24, it should be understood that:

(C) it is too early to be really optimistic about the impact of Brexit on the economy

6. From line 25 to line 30, it should be understood that:

(B) economic authorities succeeding in scaring people and businesses about Brexit

7. From line 31 to line 37, it should be understood that:

(C) the government had to rush to fix the negative impact of the scare campaign it had engineered

8. From line 38 to line 42, it should be understood that:

(A) two major retailers claim trade was not affected by the result of the referendum

9. From line 43 to line 49, it should be understood that:

(D) brexit is likely to compound some of the existing structural problems of the British economy

10. From line 50 to line 53, it should be understood that:

(A) the referendum has forced the government to be more realistic and honest about the economy

11. From line 54 to line 58, it should be understood that:

(B) one good thing about brexit is that it is going to put an end to immigrant exploitation

12. From line to line (paragraph), it should be understood that:

(D) the writer of this op-ed thinks he was definitely right in voting for brexit

II. LEXIQUE

13. doom and gloom (line 4) means :

(C) anticipations of disaster

14. dumping (line 13) means :

(A) _selling off_

15. some caveats are in order (line 18) means :

(B) _some caution is in order_

16. scant (line 18) means :

(D) _wanting_

17. reeling from (line 22) means :

(C) _feeling the hurt from_

18. it put the wind up (line 25) means :

(A) _scared_

18. warier (line 25) means :

(C) _more cautious_

19. chill out (line 33) means :

(B) _relax_

20. health-check (line 39) means :

(C) *__opinion poll__*

21. bellwethers (line 41) means :

(A) *__guides__*

22. subdued (line 47) means :

__(B) low__

23. put the squeeze on (line 49) means :

__(B) reduce__

24. more remote (line 62) means :

(D) *__more unlikely__*

III. COMPETENCE GRAMMATICALE

25.

(D) *__low-cost labour has allowed British businesses to thrive so far__*

26.

(C) *__The result of the brexit referendum has taken the government by surprise__*

27.

(C) *The referendum took place nearly 4 months ago*

28.

(A) *No sooner was the result made official than the pound dropped sharply*

29.

(B) *the voter turnout was high, with fewer people abstaining than in 1975.*

30.

(D) *the turnout among young people was much higher than had been anticipated*

31. The refugee crisis influenced the vote. It was...

(D) *one crisis too many*

32. The referendum has undoubtedly had great bearing on ...

(B) *British politics*

33. Experts deem... another referendum will be scheduled

(C) *it likely that*

34. It could take place as soon as the dust... a bit

(D) *has settled*

35. the result … different if the financial crisis...

(A) *would have been … hadn't happened*

36.

(C) *The May Cabinet is only provisional, the Tories will soon elect another leader*

37. Senior Tories, many... campaigned for 'Leave', are embarrassed at the result

(C) *of whom*

38. It is only a few months … the vote took place but it feels like ages

B) *since*

39. Many pessimists reckon the vote will not change...at all

(A) *anything*

CORRIGÉ SUJET MINES-PONTS N°1: EXPRESSION ÉCRITE

Question 1 : According to the article, what has Baidu brought to the world of data mining ? Answer the question in your own words (80 words +/- 10 percent)

Baidu is China's main location-based search engine, and its contribution to the world of data mining has just come in the shape of two innovations. The first is invaluable new research on the use of location data to predict trends in consumption and employment, based on data collected from some 600 million users, and the other is the openness : Baidu actually took the risk to publicize its undertaking, thereby making it plain that location services can be used to collect data on users for scientific purposes. (87 words)

Question 2 : « *one issue still remains – whether we really want just a few large web companies to control the power they wield through this data* ». Comment on this quotation from the article (180 words +/-10 percent)

I have mixed feelings about research such as the project Baidu has started. On the one hand, one should be wary of the surveillance potential that location-based search engines like Google hold. There is no gainsaying individuals may be spied on thanks to their cell phones ; but on the other hand, one has the choice to use or not use those services ; besides, big data is so huge that it's no longer individual, it belongs to the realm of statistics, which can bring such improvements to our lives that the issue requires pondering before we call all this another case of « Big Brother ».

Now, of course, the issue of private companies using public data is a serious one. But we needn't be paranoid about it. Private companies will seek profit, we know it, but their profits come with ours, otherwise it all falls through. Baidu is using its data for what I reckon is the public good, so I'm quite optimistic about such future use of location-based information on a large scale, even if one could object that Baidu is probably under control from the government. But then, is Google really independent ? (197 words)

CORRIGÉ SUJET MINES-PONTS N°1: THÈME

To cut a long story short (1) that's why (2) I happened to be (3) at Paris Austerlitz railway station. (...) Eventually I felt that someone was tapping my shoulder, it took some time because I was really focused, and when I am, a mammoth could roll over on my sneakers and I just would take no notice. I turned round/around.

'(have) you got a fag?'

She wore dirty (4)khaki trousers, an old jacket with holes at the elbows, a Benetton scarf like the one my mother keeps at the bottom of her cupboard as a relic (5) of her younger days (6)

'No, I'm sorry, I don't smoke. I ('ve) got mint (chewing) gums if you like.'

She pouted, and then held out her hand, I gave her the whole pack, she dropped (7) in her bag.

'Hi, I'm No. What's your name ?'

'No ? '

'Yes '

'I'm Lou – Lou Bertignac. '

'I've seen you here before several times. What are you up to (8)?'

'I come to look at people.'

(1)*variante*: in a nutshell (2)*var*: how (3)*var*: I was (4)*var*: scruffy (5)*var*: reminder /memento (6) *var*: youth (7)*var*: shoved (8)*var*: What are you doing?

CORRIGÉ SUJET MINES-PONTS N°2: EXPRESSION ÉCRITE

Question 1 : Why are BEREC's guidelines considered a 'triumph' by activists ? (80 words +/- 10 percent)

BEREC's guidelines have made very specific some principles which were hitherto ambiguous about net neutrality. Their existence entails a ban on practices that could have initiated a 'two-tier', or 'two-speed' internet ; internet service providers could have been tempted to favour profitable traffic by making it faster, at the expense of other traffic ; with these regulations, an open, free, democratic internet is protected, as only very few specific services and circumstances are exempted from the rules, and no app or service can achieve monopoly.(85 words)

Question 2 : Do you think net neutrality is important ? Why ? Support your point with examples (180 words +/- 10)

In my view, net neutrality is all-important, actually it is the *essence* of the internet ; we all know how critical is is to have a fast connection, and there are already inequalities due to differences in connections across the globe, where there exists a 'digital divide' between rural and urban areas, and between countries; given the extraordinary potential of the internet for access to knowledge and democracy, and the formidable tool for empowerment that it represents, I think internet should by all means remain the way it is, that is never prioritize traffic.

Now it is of course understandable that ISPs should expect a return on their investments, and attempt to give priority to more valuable trafic. For instance, Facebook's Aquila project, which would bring internet to rural areas, would initially offer access to a restricted number of services; that is why some activists are objecting to the venture. I think limits should always be temporary. It is criticical for the net to remain free and equal, because ultimately the real 'wealth' of the net is brought to it by its users in the form of free content, and not by its providers. (195 words)

CORRIGÉ SUJET MINES-PONTS N°2: THÈME

I gave (1) my mother a hand, I dried (2) the lettuce and mixed (3) the dressing, while listening to the three of them gossiping (4) about Mrs So-and-so who had made a scene (5) at the chemist's (6), and Mr X who had been diagnosed with prostate cancer ; with my mother commenting (7) as the case might be, 'She should be ashamed of herself for behaving like that, this is just not done (8)', or 'What a shame (9), he is so young – '. For my part, I remained silent (10) I hated that chitchat (11).

I kept just as quiet throughout (12) the meal, at which my father presided, as always. From time to time I glanced at Pierre (13), who was so much at home (14) with my family, although they were so dull and totally unlike what I longed for (15). To fight boredom (16) I served (at table), as I had when I was the girl of the house (…) as I walked back to the table with the cheese plate, one of my sisters-in-law turned to me (17):

'Iris, your dress is just stunning (18)! Where did you find it (19)?'

I smiled at her, finally feeling Pierre's eyes settle on me (20).

'I found it in my attic.'

    (1) *variante:* I lent (2) *var:* spin-dried (3)*var:* made (4)*var:* chattering (5)*var:* made a fuss/raised the roof (6) *var:* pharmacy (7)*var:* chiming in (8)*var:* you just don't do these things/one just doesn't do these things (9)*var:* how unfortunate (10) *var:* I kept quiet (11)*var:* gossip-mongering/gossiping (12)*var:* during (13)*var:* I occasionally glanced (14)*var:* in his element/in his world (15) *var:* what I could have wished for (16)*var:* to amuse myself (17) *var:* said to me/called out to me (18)*var:* magnificent/gorgeous (19)*var:* /get it from/buy it (20)*var:* /as I felt Pierre's look/eyes/ on me at last (21) *var:* it came from my attic

CORRIGÉ SUJET MINES-PONTS N°3: EXPRESSION ÉCRITE

Question 1 : Why does Paul Krugman suggest the US media is acting irresponsibly in this campaign ? (80 words +/- 10 percent, 4 points)

Paul Krugman thinks the media is overlooking what he deems to be the most consequential issue of the presidential campaign : climate change. More debates on this would be a boon for the Democratic campaign since President Obama's record on cutting emissions is good, and he has committed the US to more cuts and more clean energy use ; Mrs Clinton will keep the same line, whereas Mr Trump doesn't believe in the anthropocene theory ; therefore the election will considerably impact America's and the world's environmental future. (88 words)

Question 2 : Can politics impact global warming ? Illustrate your answer with relevant examples (180 words +/- 10 percent, 8 points)

It is too early to say if emission cuts really help limit temperature rise, but it is worth a try, because at worse they won't do any harm, and at best they can help curb global warming. If it works, then of course politics has an enormous bearing on the issue. It was thanks to political leadership from the US and China that the COP 21 was a success, after the relative failure of other conferences. It was also top-down political decisions that gave Germany a long lead in solar energy, an example now followed by the US, where fiscal incentives have boosted the renewable-energy sector.

Climate change is one of the few issues on which political consensus can be reached inside a country and between countries, which is why it is a shame to see it instrumentalized by some politicians; on the other hand, the notion that climate change is itself a political ploy used by some against others is also shared by millions of people, and their views matter too. Even anti-globalization activists are divided on this, so the progress of that opinion could influence the future of the fight against global warming. (195 words)

CORRIGÉ SUJET MINES-PONTS N°3: THÈME

She was in great shape (1) and had told me to meet her (2) at a café in the 1st district, one of those gorgeous venues to which crowds of tourists, who own the area, give a decadent atmosphere which she enjoyed. She soon insisted on going for a walk, in spite of the drizzle, which annoyed me, for I did not care to play holidaymakers (3) on a cold, wet autumn afternoon, but she really meant it and she eventually managed to bring me round .

'You know Franz', she said as we walked past the lines of horse carriages on the edge of St Stephen's Cathedral Square, 'there is something really interesting in those who think that Vienna is the gateway to the East'. Which made (4) me laugh in my turn.

'You shouldn't laugh; I think I'm going to write about that, about those depictions (5)
of Vienna as a *Porta Orientis*.'

(1) variante: in top shape/ in fine fettle

(2) var: she had suggested we meet/had arranged for us to meet

(3) var: I wasn't keen to play holidaymakers/vacationists

(4) var: had me laugh

(5) var: representations

Des remarques, des questions?

RETROUVEZ LA FEE PREPA SUR SON SITE

pour des mises à jour et des nouveaux sujets gratuits:

lafeeprepa.weebly.com